To my brother Bill,
who has introduced me to good ideas
for as long as I can remember

Contents

Part IV: The Golden Horizon

Preface

From the outset, I have stood in awe of the knowledge materials we have linked to in the Internet project I have had the good fortune to direct for the past four years. And it just keeps getting better. All over the world, intellect and imagination have been set loose to build Web sites to describe knowledge. Because the Internet is a new medium, there are few guidelines and preconceptions to reign in originality. There are all sorts of new tools and new ways of showing things in the Web medium. The costs are small and the techniques fairly simple. These things have combined to feed a cascade of creativity! When an imaginative expert who knows a lot about something decides to make a Web site about a favorite subject, the result is authoritative and often awesome. Thousands upon thousands of Web pages have been generated in this way, and the momentum feeds upon itself as more and more experts realize the opportunity to show what they know.

I hope this book will lead you into the wonderful world of online knowledge. It has been the most interesting experience of my life to have watched it transform from a primitive beginning into the most sophisticated cognitive environment ever known. I believe we have only seen the beginning, and that coming months and years will push past my already strained *awesome* adjective.

Judy Breck, New York City, October 2000

Acknowledgments

My heartfelt thanks to Tom Koerner and the people of Scarecrow Press for their support and help in telling this story.

It is my privilege and joy to work with seers and builders. Brett Jenkins, Kimberly Patterson, Cristina Elias, and Richard Flynn are the pioneers at the early Internet knowledge frontier who brought our Web collection into existence. Anthony Reynolds arrived in the thick of things and elevated us from collectors to weavers. Jennifer Cordi joined the team to mold our sciences with her broad vision. As this book goes to press, we continue as assemblers and curators of the matrix of Internet knowledge that is part of the bigchalk.com education destination.

An acknowledgment to believing in the future: As you read into these pages, you may be skeptical of what might seem to you my excessively positive approach to the future. Three grand enthusiasts taught me the validity of optimism, not as proponents of theory, but by their own consistently pivotal accomplishments. They are Thomas W. Evans, Bryant M. Kirkland, and U. A. Hyde. An older root for the optimism expressed in these pages was my mother's invincible conviction, which I share, in the personhood and potential of every child.

Introduction

As the twenty-first century begins, many folks are unhappy with the state of education. All the best people are working on it. There are many different theories and plans aimed at making things better. Yet, little noticed, a digital sword is cutting through the Gordian knot of the education mess. As the tangles fall away, a golden age of learning dawns. This book provides background and a tour of how seemingly intractable difficulties of human learning are unraveling before our eyes.

Bringing up kids has always been vexing, with much to do. Marcus Aurelius, portrayed in the movie *Gladiator* as the aging philosopher–emperor of Rome, describes what he learned in his youth:

> From my grandfather Verus I learned good morals and the government of my temper. From the reputation and remembrance of my father, modesty and a manly character. From my mother, piety and beneficence, and abstinence, not only from evil deeds, but even from evil thoughts; and further, simplicity in my way of living, far removed from the habits of the rich. From my great-grandfather, not to have frequented public schools, and to have had good teachers at home, and to know that on such things a man should spend liberally.[1]

Marcus's great grandfather was bashing the public schools nineteen centuries ago, and looking for another way to be sure his heir learned "stuff." Today, our schools spend a lot of time in areas where young Marcus found guidance from family. The schools are occupied with three areas of preparation of children for adulthood: nurture, acculturation, and teaching/learning academic knowledge.

Nurture is caring for and encouraging children. Crises in families, society, and schools have severely affected the upbringing of children throughout human experience. In the twentieth century, now behind us, millions of childhoods were ravaged by hunger and war. Recent decades have seen what Jonathan Kozol has so aptly called "savage inequalities." Today, schools are a source of hope and disappointment in the care for kids. We ask ourselves if perhaps schools will become primarily day care centers focused on preventing tragic neglect. Should the nurture of youngsters be the first goal of education? If this is the fundamental goal, is it not true that the satisfaction and confidence that come from learning useful knowledge are not in themselves the most enduring form of nurture? To the extent that nurture includes the acquisition of self-control and discipline, is not an idle mind the devil's workshop?

The presence of rites of passage into one's culture is universal. These rites are the expected experience for teenagers in hunter–gatherer tribes, in courts of kings, in street gangs, and during the high school senior year. Achieving the Apache headdress, the reading of the Torah at bar mitzvah, and the moving of the tassel on graduation day all signify thresholds crossed into particular cultures. Fulfilling the human need to belong and fit in is fundamental to our individual and social stability. It is a good thing, and something schools provide—often these days supplying a passage no longer available from family, church, or nation. Has cultural stability become the most important goal of education? If this is so, is it not true that part of earning a mature place in every culture has always included learning to do something well? Once, that could be throwing a spear or building a house. Fitting into the global culture of the new century requires working with one's head, not just with one's back or hands.

There is a tacit assumption that kids go to school to learn something once described as "reading, writing, and arithmetic," and one's ABCs. This stuff has been called academic knowledge, based on the word *academy*, which means school. It is knowledge that is appropriate to learn in school, and it is much more than the basics. Higher education calls itself "the academy." Graduate schools teach academic knowledge at the furthest levels of detail, complexity, and discovery. In the first chapter, I arbitrarily call the stuff of academic knowledge "good ideas." Stuff from multiplication tables to molecular biology and from the explorations of Cabeza de Vaca to the writings of Geoffrey Chaucer are in this book referred to interchangeably as *knowledge*, *good ideas*, and *ideas*. Common sense says, of course, that more is taught in school than what is narrowly defined as ideas. There is opinion, application, practice, and physical education. But what goes on in school does not tell us what knowledge is. The subject of this book is knowledge as defined in *Merriam-Webster's*: "the sum total of what is known: the whole body of truth, fact, information, principles or other objects of cognition acquired by humankind."[2]

This book is the story of the migration of this sort of knowledge into new media, and its spectacular digital future now emerging. To the extent that the imparting of knowledge/good ideas to students is the goal of the education establishment, schools will be formed in the future by the Grand Idea described by this book.

If I just tell you our greatest age of knowing has begun, you will probably be skeptical. If you are more generous, you will say: *I don't know what you are talk-*

ing about. The Internet is difficult to use, even for the most initiated; it is primitive, yet maturing very fast. There are dark descriptions of pornography, and the values of stocks are banged around like squash balls. Tech is king, business is boss. The jargon is jolting, and a lot of the people who use the Internet are licking the icing, not forking the cake. One of the great surprises that will soon emerge from the confusing, seemingly impenetrable Internet of today will govern the shape of future education across the planet. It is being formed from a very small percentage of the total pages on the Internet and is the subject of this book. The combination of these very special pages will become a web within the Web, and it is a grand idea indeed.

The words used in the digital world are not all jargon. Some have entered the language, or are in the process of doing so. The distinction between two of the major terms seems to be blurring. The *Internet* and the *Web* have become, for all intents and purposes, synonymous, although technically the World Wide Web forms only part of the Internet. The terms *Web site* and *Web pages* have come to mean any site that accesses the Internet. *Web authoring* designates the new process and profession of creating Web sites. It has become common practice to use the terms *Internet* and *Web*, and their variations, interchangeably. That is what I have done in this book.

My own realization of the Grand Idea developed over many months, not from theorizing, but from exploring the Internet, site by site and page by page. The awareness grew in my mind of how strikingly parallel the growth of knowledge on the Internet was to the growth of human knowledge over the thousands of years of human experience. It clarified my understanding of what I was watching on the Internet to recall how ideas were handled in earlier media, and the first three chapters set out a brief framework of ideas in the days before digital technology. The Great Change section that follows is an effort to explain that for all the jargon, a very few simple factors underlie the advent of the Internet and anyone can understand them. The last three chapters of this section describe stunning new resources and tools for education that are now multiplying in cyberspace. The last of these describes the final technical shift to wireless, which is completing the Great Change.

The last chapter of the book looks beyond the digital dawn where we now are. It contains my prediction of the inevitable formation of the Grand Idea. Although the Grand Idea has implications far beyond education, among its most important early effects will be that, inside and outside of the schools, our kids will learn more of the good ideas possessed by humankind and that teaching will be more fun. Tangles in education will be cleaved as we all connect with good ideas in new ways. The knowledge described here as good ideas is nurturing us and opening the virtual doors to a new knowing culture. Aristotle began his *Metaphysics:* "All men by their very nature feel the urge to know." Our greatest age of knowing has begun.

1

A Good Idea

Relax: you do not have to worry about theories to enjoy this book. The fact is that the conclusion of this book cannot be reached through a logical outline. New ideas are always paradigm shifts that bring together thoughts from here and there in unanticipated ways that are seldom linear or logical. New patterns that rise up out of old ideas leap to mind as wholes, and we say: *eureka*. You may be a parent or teacher with little understanding of the Internet. You may be a sophisticated programmer or technical expert. You may be just interested in the future. Whatever your frame of reference, I hope this somewhat anecdotal trip through the history of human ideas will connect a useful web of thought for you, from which you may gain insight into the beautiful new web of human ideas that is now forming within the Internet.

The tale begins with adventures of mirrors for ideas reflected from the brain. The story is as old as humankind. An amazing new chapter is unfolding before our eyes as digital media are emerging to connect, and then to reflect back to us, everything we know. In this discussion, the word *idea* refers only to a piece of thought in a mind, or to that same idea expressed in a medium. Scads of books have been written over the centuries about how the brain mirrors reality. This book gives a history of the opposite process: how reality has been used to mirror human thought. The brand-new virtual reality is the most wonderful mirror of all.

As you read, please assume the existence of reality and of thought; you should ignore the mysteries of whether and how we know. Put on blinders to the many provocative concepts treated herein with a very light touch. The goal in these pages is not to be profound, but to be simple enough to unveil a magnificent new phenomenon. To avoid getting bogged down, drop your philosophical baggage and skip like a water strider across deep pools of intriguing speculation. We will hop around to relate several things happening in the real world. We do not climb a tree or chase down ramifications: we connect a web.

An idea is a piece of thought. *Merriam-Webster's Collegiate Dictionary* includes this definition of idea: "what exists in the mind as a representation."[1] An idea can be a very useful thing; without ideas, there can be no thinking. Bad ideas can be wasteful and destructive. At the extreme, Adolf Hitler's idea of Aryan supremacy excused torture and genocide. Regretfully, human history has been tarnished by many bad ideas. We could stop here to investigate the morality of ideas, but let us move on to focus only on good ideas.

High on the facade of the New York Public Library are words of one of the great collection's founders, John Jacob Astor: "for the advancement of useful knowledge." Utility is an important aspect of a good idea. But there is another way to look at the matter, and that is by evaluating an idea's structure. Doing so sheds some insight into how ideas might inhabit the mind. Most brains contain at least a few paragraphs: perhaps the Gettysburg Address or the preamble to the Declaration of Independence. There may be a few poems stored away, and the multiplication tables can usually be found. But ideas have a form more elementary than sentences and number formulas.

Ideas come into being by connecting things. A young child may acquire the idea of a tree by developing an area of awareness of tall things, another area of things that make shade, another area of leaves, and another area of things colored green. The connecting of these points of knowing form a beginning idea of a tree. So far, it is a good idea because it is connecting things that form a mirror of something real. The baby's idea becomes structurally bad when something gets connected that does not make sense. If baby connects the awareness of wheels to the concept of a tree, at best he or she has a very weird tree. The baby does not have a good idea of a tree.

Another example of putting random pieces together to make something bigger and better comes from a new description of the early structuring of life: "early cells, each having relatively few genes, differed in many ways. By swapping genes freely, they shared various of their talents with their contemporaries. Eventually, this collection of eclectic and changeable cells coalesced into the three basic domains [bacteria, archaea, and eukaryotes] known today."[2]

Like the baby developing his or her idea of a tree, the plastic primordial cells tried different relationships of internal parts until an excellent combination jelled. Our baby will reject the wheel as part of his or her idea of a tree and will then have a good idea of a tree.

Paradigm shifts in holistic perceptions cause the whole to become more than the sum of its parts. A classic example is the blind men who are taken one by one to observe an elephant. The first places his arms around a leg. The next feels the animal's tail. Another offers a peanut that is taken through the trunk. Another feels the ivory tusks. A later discussion among these observers is fruitless because they have no way to connect the different, independently observed aspects elephantine. Each has a structurally bad idea of an elephant: it is like a tree trunk, a snake, a hose that sucks, a hard cylinder. The miracle of thought is our grasp of pattern and structure that lets us know an elephant from the relations among his parts. Having a good idea means the mind has understood the integrated structure of parts as a whole. Rudolf Arnheim points out that "the mind always functions as a whole. All perceiving is also thinking, all reasoning is also intuition, all observation is also invention."[3]

The mind is very good at grasping relevant points out of chaos, connecting them, and coming up with something more than just a bunch of pieces. Seeing and thinking do that all the time. Primitive ideas can be visualized in white clouds against a blue sky. Cloud structures can resonate with ideas of ships and monkeys and Santa Claus. As a boy, Leonardo da Vinci honed his drawing skills by perceiving and sketching fanciful creatures from the random structures of the underbrush. Gesture drawing is connecting the kinetic structure of a model so as to draw what the figure is doing. Art can be defined as a reflection of the ideas artists observe. *Iso-* means equal; *morph* means form. Art is isomorphic: equal in form to the ideas it seeks to express.

Good ideas can be very simple, and they can be very rich. Take the eight-note musical idea from Beethoven's Fifth Symphony that became a World War II battlefield signal. Those eight notes alone are expressive, yet they can occupy dozens of instruments throughout the playing of the entire symphony. Rich chords embellish the melody. The idea of a tree will grow in the infant's mind through observation and experience. As a youngster, he may learn favorite limbs to climb. He may come to savor his memory of a tree in the moonlight from the night he proposed to his wife. In late life, his concept of tree could partake of forests where he has traveled, books he read over many decades, and botanical sciences he learned. Each of the points he originally connected to first think of a tree would by now have connected to many other ideas. Tall things now connect to skyscrapers and basketball players, leaves suggest rustling sounds, shade conjures gardens and coolness, and green has a place in thousands of ideas.

Does everybody need to know everything about trees that the old man came to know? The answer is, obviously, no. There is a richness of personal memories and observations unique to each person. No means of communication would allow each person to know every idea of each other person. Every person has also processed many ideas that were temporarily useful, like one's daily bank balance, but which fade from memory. The whole of what a mature person knows is a wondrous web—a gift of age and personal discipline of thoughtfulness. If you keep acquiring and processing ideas into your later years, you become eloquent: able to say the same thing in several ways. After decades of assuming that the brain does not keep producing cells for thinking, recent work suggest that new neurons develop every day. As new cells move into the regions of higher thought, good ideas can keep coming at any age.

Are all the ideas that are good for our old man good for everyone? Yes and no. By the structural definition above, a good idea has a good structure. Thus, any structurally good idea the old man has should work for you and for anyone else. So, yes, all of his good ideas are good for everybody. But measuring ideas by usefulness, the answer often becomes no. Sound as his idea was in 1984 for constructing new stairs for his basement, you are unlikely to find it useful—unless you have a similar basement. If it is a good idea, you could use it.

Are there good ideas everybody should know? The answer to that is yes. There are good ideas everybody must know, good ideas most people should know, and good ideas only a few people ever get to know. These three can be looked at as stages in human development. There are good ideas that everyone needs to survive. There are good ideas that have been developed over the course of human history. And there are good ideas at the frontiers of thinking, ones that are shaping the future. You need to know the first kind to function. The amount you get of the second kind plays a big role in your personal progress. The more people who have the third kind in any era, the more golden is that age.

The ideas everybody must know include things such as fire burns and the stove is hot. Urban kids have to learn not to chase balls into traffic. Rural kids have to learn not to wander into forests. A minimal vocabulary, knowing the colors, and other basics are, of course, crucial. Words reflect ideas: the word *elephant* means nothing unless it provokes the mind to recall the structural relations of parts that make the whole elephant idea come to mind.

Beyond the ideas needed for survival stretch the good ideas that humankind has developed over the millennia. They range from counting and arithmetic to plate tectonics and telerobotics—with a very great deal in between. You can learn enough through a simple world history time line of five thousand years to avoid embarrassment at cocktail parties, or you can devote a lifetime to studying a single archaeological site. You can learn just enough chemistry to get a laboratory job, or keep on learning chemistry until you develop a drug that cures a disease. The good ideas that few people ever get to know tend to belong to those who have won the privilege by thinking about and persistently probing the unknown. But if it is a particularly practical new idea, the whole world may share it very fast, whether it be the cure for polio, automated teller machine (ATM) banking, or hesitating windshield wipers.

As we will see, it is already easier than it has ever been for every person everywhere to acquire every sort of good idea. A coming paradigm shift will make the Grand Idea available to all. The coming chapters outline how that has happened, what the Grand Idea will be, and how it will golden our new century.

We begin with what we have done as a species to get the good ideas we have inside our heads over into the heads of fellow humans.

NOTES

1. *Merriam-Webster's Collegiate Dictionary*, 10th ed., 1997.

2. W. Ford Doolittle, "Uprooting the Tree of Life," *Scientific American,* vol. 282, February 2000, 95.

3. Rudolf Arnheim, *Art and Visual Perception* (Berkeley: University of California Press, 1974), 5.

II

CLUMSY COMMUNICATION

Media bashing is fair game these days. The fact is that, as a species, we are only pretty good at letting other people know what we are thinking and awkward at spreading the word about what is happening. As a prelude to appreciating the Great Change now occurring in communication across every medium, we first take an informal look at the spotty record of human communication.

call has received a very useful idea from outside of her own head—reflected from
the bird's call. She is able to act upon it in more than one way. Knowing of the
cat's ability to enter the garden, she can build her next home inside the shed ceiling. But just as Papa Squirrel had no way to describe the two-peanut carrying
method abstractly to his son, Mother Mouse cannot describe any details of her
good idea of building a ceiling nest to a pregnant daughter. Her suite of mirrors
that she can use to reflect thoughts to her young probably goes little beyond hardwired generalities like the jay's call. Because mother mice can give birth to as
many as a hundred babies in a year, genetic selection works better than maternal
squeak lectures, even if Mama could keep in touch with all her children.

The point here is not that creatures other than humans cannot communicate.
Quite the contrary: communication with other individuals may be a universal trait
of living beings, beginning with chemocommunication in the oldest and most
primitive organisms known. But as a first step toward understanding the elegant
new communication our species will experience, we look at the fundamental difference between mice and men: the suite of mirrors humans have devised for reflecting what they know from other humans.

It is my view that ideas form in the head first, and the ways to communicate
them have to be learned—beyond at least our earliest gurgles. The gurgles themselves may be primitive attempts to create something by which Mama can understand the ideas we are forming. Over the years I have coached and judged a lot of
young teenagers in competitive debate. It is marvelous to watch plastic young
minds test out their developing logical skills and practice learning to say what they
are thinking. The effective articulation of ideas in high school debate requires
enough vocabulary to make sensible explanations and arguments. Once when I
was coaching some kids at a poorly functioning high school, I paired off four of
them into teams of two and gave them ten minutes to prepare arguments, two on
the affirmative and two on the negative, to debate the question of whether students
should be required to wear uniforms to school. On debate teams from the worst
schools, one usually encounters young people with very high intelligence and su-
perbly developed survival skills. On the particular occasion of the quickly prepared debate on an issue the kids felt strongly about, I watched the brightest boy
of the four nearly explode, clinging white-knuckled to the lectern. Finally he ex-
claimed, "I know what this argument is, but I don't know how to say it!" He did
not have enough dexterity with the English language to tell us what he was thinking. Human language has developed over time into a complex tool by which we
articulate ideas from our minds, reflecting them into the minds of others.

Human language is seldom perfect, and it can sometimes utterly fail. An example is this sad story from the days when slaves were rounded up for sale from
African villages. As the slavers approached the remote interior, an African from
the seacoast managed to move ahead of the raiding party. He ran through village
after village crying, "The slavers are coming! The slavers are coming!" The local
people would look up from their chores or pleasures to watch the running man,

then return to what they had been doing. The slavers entered the villages one by one and took away all of the able-bodied people. The exhausted man who had sounded the alarm watched from the brush in horror. He finally sat with a weeping grandmother left in an almost empty village. As he described to the old woman what was going to happen to her people, he learned from her that the villagers had not understood the warning because they had no word for slave. Language is the first great mirror of ideas from one human head to another. Think about the word slave. What reflections appear in your mind?

Language reflects ideas out of the head and puts them into a new medium of words and relationships. There is a lot of fascinating work under way in linguistics and related fields that explores the rich subject of language. We identify language here as a first and powerful mirror for ideas independent of any particular mind. Words contain meaning. We assign ideas we have to words so that we can share those ideas with other people.

Linguist Steven Pinker begins his book *Words and Rules* by pointing out: "Language comes so naturally to us that it is easy to forget what a strange and miraculous gift it is. All over the world members of our species fashion their breath into hisses and hums, and squeaks and pops and listen to others do the same."[1] When Pinker explains that grammar is a "combinatorial system, in which a small inventory of elements can be assembled by rules into an immense set of distinct objects,"[2] there is an echo to the structure of good ideas. It is not doing the same thing here as forming ideas, exactly, but different points are being related to generate patterns. But we are getting prematurely caught up in webs.

Language is a mirror for the ideas that originate in somebody's head at some point. Language can be used to reflect large and complex ideas in the form of oral traditions. The second chapter of Genesis tells us: "And the Lord God planted a garden eastward of Eden; and there he put the man he had formed. And out of the ground made the Lord God to grow every tree that is pleasant to the sight, and good for food; the tree of life also in the midst of the garden, and the tree of knowledge of good and evil. And a river went out of Eden to water the garden. . . ."[3]

There are many ideas set out in these words. Out of whose head did those ideas come, and how did they come down to us, over a period of at least five thousand years? If we take the Bible literally, the ideas are observations of Adam and his immediate descendants, who saw the garden and the trees with their own eyes. As far as we know, they had no writing materials to record the happenings. So they would have used spoken language to pass the story from generation to generation, a practice better known as oral tradition.

Those who choose not to take the Bible literally can conjecture that when Abraham came up from Ur, he remembered Mesopotamia as the garden of the Fertile Crescent. He described the garden of his past to his children, and they described it to theirs. Perhaps that is the origin of the garden's description, which by the Jewish calendar is some 5,760 years old. Genesis continues: "The Lord God sent him forth from the garden of Eden, to till the ground from whence he was taken."[4] This could be the memory of people who had once lived in a verdant river valley, but moved out into the nomadic life, tending their flocks and tilling different ground in different seasons. By a literal interpretation of the biblical text, however, the Garden of Eden was a particular place in the Fertile Crescent of six millennia ago. Other traditions and cultures cherish narrations of creation and flood similar to those in the Bible. Three close cousins work together to mirror these ancient ideas: oral traditions, stories, and narration. The account of the garden contains ideas of religion, morality, and agriculture, as well as history.

Fields of scholarship that explore history through literature study the mirror of narration. Hayden White introduces a discussion of the value of narrativity in the representation of reality with these words of Roland Barthes:

> Narrative "is simply there like life itself . . . international, transhistorical, transcultural." Far from being a problem, then, narrative might well be considered a solution to a problem of general human concern, namely, the problem of how to translate knowing into telling, the problem of fashioning human experience into a form assimilable to structures of meaning that are generally human rather than culture-specific.[5]

Leaving the garden was undoubtedly a frequent experience for our hunter–gatherer ancestors, and the story still holds us with its beauty and remorse.

Modern people are used to looking into the mirror of historical writing to get ideas of what happened in the past. Being able to do that is relatively new. The writing of history came along dozens of generations after the story of the garden had begun to be told from parent to child. We are so used to being able to look up history we fail to appreciate that the Father of History, Herodotus, lived three thousand years after the births of the first civilizations, in Egypt, Mesopotamia, India, and China. The Hebrews recorded their history because they saw God as active there. Through their faith and scholarship, they have always viewed as historical facts the stories of the life of King David (whom modern historians affirm was alive in the year 1000 B.C.), their Exodus from Eygpt that occurred a few centuries earlier than David's life, and the even older events of Hebrew history commencing with Abraham. But it is certain that there was no historian in the courts of the pharaohs, nor in the gardens of Babylon, nor the Indus golden age, nor in the China of Confucius.

What was the date when Abraham came up from Ur and founded the Hebrew nation? When was the Exodus when Moses led his people out of Egypt? What about ancient China: what are the details of the events by which the Shang dynasty brought about a shining bronze age, and the Chou replaced them with the feudal age? The past tells us about itself through a variety of mirrors to which historical writing is a very late comer. Those who write history in our times rely on tradition, stories, and many more tangible kinds of evidence from long-gone people who, just like us, had good ideas they wanted to express.

There are mirrors from antiquity that do not require words to reflect the ideas of even our prehistoric ancestors. The Somerset Levels in England is the site of the Sweet Track, a Neolithic raised footpath that tree-ring dating indicates was used over a period of only a decade, about four thousand years ago. The track was almost two kilometers long, crossing above the swamp that eventually created the peat moss, the modern harvest of which has revealed the remains of the structure. Sweet Track was constructed from the wood of oak, lime, and ash trees. There were 600 planks, 3,699 pegs, and 350 poles, all prefitted pieces so well designed that a practice test showed that a group of ten people could put the entire elevated footpath together in less than a day. We can marvel at the skills, planning, and teamwork that built Sweet Track. There could have been no detailed blueprint, because paper did not yet exist. The structural ideas resided in the minds of the builders. The presence of similar contemporary tracks in Europe makes it clear that the good idea of building the track was reflected from the structure itself. Somebody from Somerset must have looked carefully at a footpath elsewhere, remembered how it was built, and led the Sweet Track team.

Until about two centuries ago, oral narratives, stories, and structures are about all the direct, albeit remote, contact living people had with prehistoric ancestors. Structures were scattered about, and some remained enormously impressive. Did the people living in northern Europe have any idea what was happening in Egypt or the Fertile Crescent before Herodotus, who lived in the fifth century B.C., gave birth to the writing of history? It may be a coincidence that while the great pyramids were under construction along the Nile, Stonehenge was being set up in England. It is also possible that the idea of building big stone things radiated far in all directions from the shores of the Mediterranean Sea in that millennium. Certainly these stone monuments proved durable. Are they also monuments to the traveling power of an idea?

I do not know the answer, but I did once see a venerable monument to the mirroring of an idea over time. When visiting Egypt in 1971 with my parents, we had the good fortune to have as our guide Professor Zaki Y. Saad. When he led us through the environs of the Step Pyramid at Saqqâra, he pointed out some very old columns. He describes them in his book: "The visitor then enters the magnificent hypostyle hall. It is a long narrow passage with two rows of columns shaped like sheaves of reeds and meant to support a heavy stone-roof made of slabs and curved at their lower edge in the form of palm logs."[6]

Professor Saad pointed at the forms of the tips of the leaves spreading at the tops of the columns. He told us that these were the source of the idea of leaf shapes at the tops of columns ever since. Over three thousand years after the construction at Saqqâra, leafy capitals adorned columns in Greece. They appeared later in Rome, in the Renaissance, and in modern classical revivals. Having leafy forms at the top of columns was an idea of enormous staying power.

The events and ideas of those who set up Stonehenge were forgotten for thousands of years. Only in the twentieth century did we realize how old the monument is. In the past, the great circle of standing stones was credited to Celtic peoples, and Celtic druids were thought to have been the architects. It is now known that the Celts did not enter England until about a thousand years after the stone circle was erected. Similarly, the ideas that led to the building of the great pyramids of Egypt disappeared into the sand and were unknown to living people for at least two millennia.

Thousands of years before civilizations emerged, people of every known culture were mirroring their ideas through art. We have a drive to see what we know, and we find enormous delight in manipulating sight and sound. In rearing a child, there is relief when the stage is passed of scribbling on walls, and there is pride in framing the first finger paintings by the little ones. As they get a little older, they will tell just what their drawings are and will have stories about them. The imagination of young children lets them use the images they draw as doorways to enter the make-believe world their young minds enjoy.

Art can mirror profound and sophisticated ideas. In what Kenneth Clark has called "a prodigious leap of imagination" and "a work of almost incredible originality,"[7] Donatello merged the great King David of Israel into the sculpted beauty of a god of antiquity. The beautiful, naked figure recognizable as Dionysus stands sword in hand and foot on the decapitated head of Goliath. The idea that soon became the High Renaissance—the merging of the classical and Judeo–Christian heritages—was perfectly and ineffably reflected from the mirror created by the mind and hands of the great Donatello.

There is in China a vast tomb built for Qin Shi Haungi, who became emperor at age thirteen in 246 B.C. and died in 210 B.C. Tradition reports that 700,000 workers built the vast underground structure. In 1974, Chinese peasants accidentally discovered buried rooms containing thousands of terra-cotta soldiers. A few years after the discovery, I became acquainted with the son of a high-ranking military officer of the army of the People's Republic of China. My friend had studied law at Duke University with the first group of students from the People's Republic to seek legal training in the United States. He was extremely smart and seemed to know everything about China. He had once met Mao, his father having secured an appointment for him when he was a teenager. He described his meeting in hushed terms, saying that he had felt an overpowering magnetism from the aging tyrant. My friend told me about the Qin tomb. He said that the leaders of China were wise enough to know that they did not yet have the technology to appropriately excavate this and many other archaeological sites in their vast country.

If he was right, the coming decades may well become the golden age of Chinese archaeology. Already, the terra-cotta soldiers provide a startlingly direct mirror of the time of Qin. Every one of the more than seven thousand soldiers has an individual face. Because of a long tradition of literature and government records, China's ancient people have not seemed remote, and new archaeological discoveries will fill in a story long since sketched out. But the intimacy of looking at the reflection from the face of an individual soldier is a marvelously direct mirror of a real person from another time.

Before we turn to the most effective mirror for our ideas, writing them down, there is a final nonwritten mirror of great importance. In order to appreciate the

Grand Idea that lies ahead, it needs to be clear that we are very skilled at embedding ideas in other ideas. Above all we are classifiers, because it helps keep one thing straight from another.

My college zoology textbook, published in 1951, comments that zoologists differ with respect to how many phyla there are into which animals can be classified, but that "usually 11 are studied in some detail in a beginning zoology class." The textbook contains chapters on these eleven phyla, plus a chapter on "miscellaneous minor phyla" whose "relationships to other animals and to each other are rather uncertain."[8] A biology textbook on the kingdoms of life printed in 1998 lists ninety-six phyla. Not only have the phyla counters been very busy over the last half century, but biologists have learned that the trees of life, with their origins in ideas sketched by Aristotle, are not actually found in the biota, but are heuristic mirrors constructed by scientists as tools for studying nature. The tree does not issue from or exist in nature. As the authors of the 1998 textbook explain: "Why do our concepts of classification shift through time? Every taxon—class, order, phylum, kingdom—is artificial but based on the study of relationships. We recognize that only the species is a natural taxon."[9]

The tree tool, like the tree of life onto which biologists have hung species, is very useful. In its simplest applications, it is perfect. The National Basketball Association (NBA) store on Fifth Avenue in Manhattan places a tree diagram of basketball teams, symbolized by team jerseys, in its window to keep track of the play-offs. The whole tournament is visible in a glance. The Dewey decimal system worked very well for many decades as a classification tree for cataloging the contents of libraries. The logic tree is the basis for the programming of computers. It is not only very effective to write down an idea. It is often useful to build the ideas that are to be written down into a logical outline, which is a branching of ideas just like a tree. Yet as we will see later on, there is a new and better way to mirror the organization of ideas that exists within the mind. We shall also see that the use of a mental structure based on a tree to serve as the matrix for ideas was a forerunner to the more elegant matrix that makes the Grand Idea possible.

The grandest known matrix for ideas is the human mind. Language, oral and written, reflects ideas into the listener's or reader's own theater of the mind. Twenty-four centuries ago, Herodotus wrote these words that place the Argippaens onto the reader's mental stage: "Each of them dwells under a tree, and they cover the tree in winter with a cloth of thick white felt, but take off the covering in the summer-time. No one harms these people, for they are looked upon as sacred—they do not even possess any warlike weapons. When their neighbors fall out, they make up the quarrel; and when one flies to them for refuge, he is safe from all hurt. They are called the Argippaeans."[10]

Did you think of a large, spreading tree or of a stark and bare one supporting the tent of white felt? It is more fun to write for radio than for television, because in radio the listener will add her own details to what you write, appealing to the theater of the mind instead of relying on studio sets and clip art.

It would seem likely that once people invented ways to write things down, all ideas could be mirrored in written form. Writing records the idea mirror of language and represents that mirror in intelligible form to readers. Stories were scratched in clay. Oral traditions were inscribed on papyrus and paper. Laws were chiseled into stone. The exploits of kings were written on the walls of their monuments and tombs. Yet it has never been certain that saying or writing a good idea assures that anyone else will get the reflection from these individual mirror tools—nor that if anyone does, the idea will not be lost later on. As the next chapter describes, the media have to gather and spread ideas, and media's success record, to be generous, is partial.

Writing and reading, just like speaking and listening, are playing integral roles in the Great Change and the Grand Idea. They are key tools of individual teachers and students, who are already beginning to use these tools in a brand-new medium—a medium that represents a major leap forward toward mirroring the way our minds structure ideas.

NOTES

1. Steven Pinker, *Words and Rules* (New York: Basic, 1999), 1.

2. Pinker, *Words*, 7.

3. Genesis 2:8–10 King James Version.

4. Genesis 3:23.

5. Hayden White, "The Value of Narrativity in the Representation of Reality," in *On Narrative,* edited by W. J. T. Mitchell (Chicago: University of Chicago Press, 1980), 1. Roland Barthes, "Introduction to the Structural Analysis of Narratives," in *Image, Music, Text*, trans. Stephen Heath (New York: Hill and Wang, 1977), 79.

6. Zaki Y. Saad, *Pharaonic Egypt Guide* (Cairo: Anglo-Egyptian Bookshop, 1964), 40.

7. Kenneth Clark, *The Nude* (Princeton: Princeton University Press, 1956), 54.

8. Robert W. Hegner and Karl A. Stiles, *College Zoology,* 6th ed. (New York: Macmillan, 1951), 2.

9. Lynn Margulis and Karlene V. Schwartz, *Five Kingdoms* (New York: Freeman, 1998), xvii.

10. Herodotus, *The Histories,* Book 4, trans. George Rawlison. *Great Books—Texts and Fully Searchable Concordances* <www.concordance.com/herodotus.htm> [accessed 23 October 2000].

3

Media

The media lost Atlantis. It was a blockbuster story, that much we know, because an entire civilization disappeared under the sea. Perhaps it was just a city, but that still would have made fantastic film footage, and the stories of tragedy could have been spun out for months and years. It seems likely that there really was an Atlantis disaster and that the media of the day did cover the story thoroughly, causing the echo of the catastrophe still coming down to us today. Perhaps what caused the memory was the dramatic eruption of the Santoríni Volcano in the seventeenth century B.C., a gigantic explosion on a small eastern Mediterranean island during the Bronze Age of the Minoan civilization. Atlantis was already a remote report at the time of Plato, who has Critias explain to Socrates that Atlantis was once an island larger than Libya and Asia, but now lay sunk by earthquakes.[1] Critias gives as his source his great-grandfather, Dropides, who was a friend and relative of the great Solon, who told it to Dropides. When he traveled to the Nile delta, Solon had obtained a written report of the disappearance of Atlantis from Egyptian priests.

The media of thirty-seven centuries ago was a lot slower than media is today. Blanketing the world with the news of the disappearance of Atlantis would have taken months and years. That is quite a contrast to the coverage a few years ago of the enormous eruption of Mount St. Helens in the state of Washington. Cameras were trained on the mountain for days in advance. Anyone with a television set could watch the mountain pour debris into the sky in real time. As soon as it was fairly safe, news crews spread out over the disaster, broadcasting everything they found to the world.

Media's role is to gather and then to broadcast. These jobs suggest an aspect of how our brains work: "An important principle of brain organization [is] that the output of a neuron is fractionated, as it were, through many synapses onto many other neurons, and, conversely, that synapses from many sources connect to a given neuron. This is referred to as divergence and convergence, respectively. It is an essential aspect of the complexity of information processing in the brain."[2] *Divergence* and *convergence* are also used in broadband networking. As we shall see later on, an enriched complexity of information handling is a gift of the Internet to human thought and education. The words *divergence* and *convergence* describe this complexity. They have been picked up in the vocabulary of networking technology because that world is *hyper*, meaning that anything can connect to anything, going in any and every direction. The hyperworld is an environment of connectivity where, like in the brain, things do not simply spread out or contract (broadcast and gather), but they diverge and converge in all sorts of interesting ways, like a tangled web. The neurology textbook explains that the brain is hardwired to allow signals to diverge and converge to and from countless points. Computer networks diverge and converge in a similar way. Ideas seem to flow in the mind to diverge as we ponder and converge as we bring relationships into focus. I use *diverge* and *converge* often in the pages ahead. I continue to introduce, them because the flow of ideas has always been more than broadcasting and gathering and soon will be very much more. Throughout history, what has been known has diverged across distance and time, and converged in specific locales, as we will discuss next. Later we will look at divergence and convergence in hypertechnologies and the exciting new realm of digitally reflected knowledge.

In the previous chapter, we examined how an individual could think an idea and then use a mirror of some sort to reflect that thought to another person. Media goes the steps beyond one-to-one communication. Media diverges ideas to many, and converges the ideas of many. Cable News Network (CNN) broadcasts what its news teams gather. To put into perspective the innovations and value of the Great Change coming up, the exciting potential for better media systems should be kept in mind against the clumsy and haphazard methods of the past. Losing a city under the sea is just one example of the way ideas have spread out yet faded into obsurity. We will also look at a haunting failure to make ideas come together usefully. The troubles of media up to now are not pretty—but the way the Grand Idea diverges and converges what is known is going to be gorgeous.

In the history of human media, divergence came first, and much later media began to work on converging what was known. The first media for spreading ideas afar were diasporas and migrations. As we discussed in the preceding chapter, when people left the garden of their early origin, they took their memories with them. As they multiplied and dispersed, these memories went with them to new places and new generations. The Bible includes several peoples of Canaan and mentions both their diversity and their absorption into other creeds and tribes.

A new theme in the study of diasporas is a fast-developing field of genetics, anthropology, and history. *The Search for Eve,* Michael H. Brown's 1990 bestseller, aroused public awareness of a paradigm shift in the study of human origins. Quoting Brown:

> It is enough to make any paleoanthropologist breathe heavily: Finally, by use of some
> of the more complex techniques known to science, we knew how modern man arose.
> Finally, a common ancestor of every living being had been located—and of all

places, in a test tube! . . . A single woman whose genes had survived through the centuries. It was a eureka moment: she lived about 200,000 years ago, probably on the savannahs of South or East Africa.[3]

These early genetic explorations were done with mitochondrial DNA, which continues through the maternal line from generation to generation. Not only occurrences of diaspora were proven. In 1996 the DNA of England's Cheddar Man, the corpse discovered in 1903 of a young man who died at the end of the last Ice Age, was tested against DNA provided by volunteers from the Cheddar area. A close match to the DNA of a local schoolteacher gave proof that at least one local family had stayed put for around ten thousand years.

In the spring of 2000, the *New York Times* reported work that suggests the human family had ten Adams and eighteen Eves.[4] The consensus in these fascinating studies holds that our forebears originated in Africa and spread across the continents. Other theories hold that, like the primordial cells of early life, things may well have been more plastic than a discrete family tree begun by a few *homo sapiens* coming out of Africa less than 200,000 years ago. Some of our ancestors may have wandered into Neanderthal camps and fallen in love with the cut of their brows. *Homo erectus* folk were scattered across the globe, and they could have been conquered by assimilation as well as annihilation. The advance of genetic science promises new knowledge in coming years. The web of relationships woven by our distant ancestors will come into clearer view.

Diaspora and migrations in historic times are better documented, though the details are not all established. There was the Dorian invasion of Greece and the Aryan invasion of India. Time and again, people moved east into China from central Asia. The Vikings made contact in Nova Scotia with the descendants of people who had moved across Asia into and across North America. Alexander swept across the Middle East and into India, spreading Hellenic culture. Caesar conquered Gaul, beginning the Latinizing of France and Germany. The Jews were taken in captivity to Babylon and later dispersed across the Mediterranean world and beyond. Romans invaded Britain, withdrew, and left the bonnie islands to be invaded by Angles, Saxons, Vikings, and Normans. The Roman Empire fell to the barbarians. Eastern hordes swept across Asia into Europe. Islam marched across North Africa and into Spain. Europeans set sail to explore the world. Slavery triggered the tragic diaspora of Africans. Manifest Destiny was fulfilled as Native Americans were replaced by American settlers. Europe colonized the world. The colonized world rejected empire.

With every move traveled the ideas of the people in motion. The movement of people from earliest times served as the major medium for dispersing ideas. When you set off seeking greener pastures, or when you were hauled off into slavery, you took your ideas with you.

A study by Gwendolyn Midio Hall of the African captives who were brought to Louisiana before 1730 indicates that they were from the Senegambia area of

West Africa, in contrast to other African ethnic groups that went to the American eastern seaboard. A *New York Times* report on Dr. Hall's work states, "The culture [the Senegambians] brought with them—music, language, food, folklore—became the foundation of Louisiana's distinctive Creole culture, a way of life for both whites and blacks for hundreds of years to this day. 'Even Uncle Remus stories were originally Wolof folktales which were first written down in Louisiana,' Dr. Hall said, referring to one of the Senegambian ethnic groups."[5] The people themselves were the medium that carried what they knew to distant shores.

But moving people is not all that efficient as a way of spreading ideas. Although the Wolof stories endure, at least to some degree, one can only wonder how many African cultures were lost in the great diaspora. Many good ideas disappeared in the plagues that reduced America's native tribes. Attila the Hun may have imposed some Hunnish culture on the Roman Empire, but some classical literature disappeared in the conflagrations. We will see that the Grand Idea offers the promise of both preserving all that is known now and of resurrecting much that is lost. But we get ahead of the story.

Very early on, a big problem for dispersing knowledge to everybody was recognized:

> And the whole earth was of one language, and of one speech. And it came to pass, as they journeyed from the east, that they found a plain in the land of Shinar; and they dwelt there. And they said one to another, Go to, let us make brick, and burn them thoroughly. And they had brick for stone, and slime had they for mortar. And they said, Go to, let us build us a city and a tower, whose top may reach unto heaven; and let us make us a name, lest we be scattered abroad upon the face of the whole earth. And the Lord came down to see the city and the tower, which the children of men builded. And the Lord said, Behold, the people is one, and they have all one language; and this they begin to do: and now nothing will be restrained from them, which they have imagined to do. Go to, let us go down, and there confound their language, that they may not understand one another's speech. So the Lord scattered them abroad from thence upon the face of all the earth: and they left off to build the city. Therefore is the name of it called Babel; because the Lord did there confound the language of all the earth: and from thence did the Lord scatter them aboard upon the face of all the earth.[6]

Of all things, this several-thousand-year-old account blames the dispersion of peoples on the confounding of language, instead of the confounding of language on the dispersion of peoples. But the memory is solid: groups of people broke off from other groups and spoke different languages. The most perfect mirror we have to tell another person our ideas became unusable except within our own language. For thousands of years, this situation just got worse. There were brief periods when a lingua franca would arise, such as Latin in the Roman world, but for the most part languages continued to diversify with geography. The impact on media was terrible. Folks in one place could not tell people in other places what they were thinking. Cultures grew in isolation.

An interesting result of the isolation was that, people being people, they all had some common challenges. How, for example, does one pick up food without using fingers? The West went with forks, the East went with chopsticks. Another preoccupation set about separately by most cultures was developing a workable calendar. The moon and the sun were shared tools available to all. There was minimal communication from Europe to Asia, as calendars were developed in China, India, Babylon, Egypt, and Rome. In magnificent isolation, the Mayans invented their great cycle calendar. Today, the atomic clock and global communications are forcing time and date keeping to converge into a single standard.

What would it have been like, and what would have happened in the history that followed, if the sort of media convergence we are accustomed to had been available when Pericles was a boy? When the great Greek who would lead the Athenian golden age was twelve years old, Confucius was fifty-four, Buddha was forty-five, and Darius I was fifty-five. What if young Pericles could have watched these world leaders and sages on a television panel? What could it have meant for the future had they been in touch with each other and with the world? But the barriers of distance and language made them unaware even of the existence of each other.

At the time of Pericles, communication on foot was the method of choice. The speed of a runner was a factor in one of history's most pivotal events, the battle of Marathon. The battle took place 26.2 miles north of Athens in 490 B.C., when Pericles was five years old. Persian King Darius had invaded Europe with an army of more than 700,000 by crossing the Bosporus on a bridge of boats. The Persians moved south through Greece, capturing and enslaving the towns north of Athens. When Athenians learned that a part of the Persian army was landing on the Plain of Marathon, they dispatched a professional runner, Pheidippides, to alert their Spartan allies 140 miles away. On the second day of his run Pheidippides reached Sparta, but they could not march. Their religious law dictated that they had to wait until after the full moon. The Athenians defeated the Persians. Herodotus describes what happened:

> So when the battle was set in array, and the victims showed themselves favorable, instantly the Athenians, so soon as they were let go, charged the barbarians at a run. Now the distance between the two armies was little short of eight furlongs. The Persians, therefore, when they saw the Greeks coming on at speed, made ready to receive them, although it seemed to them that the Athenians were bereft of their senses, and bent upon their own destruction; for they saw a mere handful of men coming on at a run without either horsemen or archers. Such was the opinion of the barbarians; but the Athenians in close array fell upon them, and fought in a manner worthy of being recorded. They were the first of the Greeks, so far as I know, who introduced the custom of charging the enemy at a run, and they were likewise the first who dared to look upon the Median garb, and to face men clad in that fashion. Until this time the very name of the Medes had been a terror to the Greeks to hear.[7]

One of the startling things about this account is the intimate picture we get from a time when communication was very primitive. The events are so important, and the story is such a good one, that the battle of Marathon has come down to us in vivid detail. Scholars have gossiped over the centuries about whether the Spartans wimped out. The one detail that makes the name of the battle familiar today was fouled up somewhere in the transmission into modern times: our competitive marathons are 26.2 miles long because that is the distance from the Plain of Marathon to the city of Athens. But Pheidippides, the runner remembered for his role on the occasion of the great battle, was an iron man: he ran 140 miles from Athens to Sparta.

This is historically certain: the defeat of the Persians at Marathon ended Persian imperialism in Greece. Although a naval battle followed at Salamis ten years later, the issue of freedom had been settled in the Greek mind at Marathon. When I visited the monument that stands on the Plain of Marathon marking the graves of the ancient heroes, a guard proudly told me that 6,400 Persians fell while "we lost only 192 men. Their remains lie here." The fire in the Athenians the day of the battle that won Greek freedom reflected from the guard's eyes. Aristotle held that Asiatics were slaves by nature, and Herodotus tells us of a Greek saying to a Persian, "You do not know what freedom is. If you did you would fight for it with your bare hands if you had no weapons." [8] The age of Pericles that followed the repulse of the Persians is unparalleled in human achievement. The Hellenic spirit was in full blossom. In the decades that tumbled into and through the next two centuries, literature, philosophy, science, medicine, and art flourished. The campaigns of Alexander the Great in the early fourth century B.C. took Hellenic treasures across the Middle East, into Egypt, and on to India. As the Roman Republic grew and became the Roman Empire, the Romans absorbed Greek ideas.

It was Will Durant, I believe, who once wrote that all of our ancestors weren't fools. History is too often taught in a superficial manner these days, and the emphasis is on processes and trends. It is difficult to cut through to the reality of those who populated our past. But they were real, and they were not all fools. For those who sensed the towering greatness of the Greek achievement of Periclean Athens, living in the century that followed must have been a letdown. Edith Hamilton wrote, "Fourth century Athens is completely overshadowed by Athens of the fifth century, so much so that it is little considered. . . . The fourth century is the introduction to a world-tragedy, the disappearance of creative power in Greece. With its close there is an end of the art and philosophy which have made a few centuries in Athens more precious to the West than many ages in many countries."[9]

Egypt had been the first intellectual giant of the Mediterranean world, and perhaps the first anywhere to invent writing. They pictured words as little icons that represented ideas. Egyptian hieroglyphics were inscribed on royal tombs. The scribal caste became highly important, and to enter into this elite required many years of training to master the thousands of glyphs and strokes. The Phoenicians have given their name to a simpler idea for writing down words: the phonetic alphabet of less than thirty symbols, each representing a sound, not an idea. It was a system anyone could learn and use, very quickly. Once the idea got around, languages through the Middle East and Europe were soon written in phonetic letters. The Egyptians acquired some phonetic symbols among their glyphs, but the scribal caste was still important and deserving of intense preparation. For whatever reason, the scribes continued to use picture writing for a thousand years after somebody thought of phonetics. Could it be that the glory of Greece could have been Egypt's if they had made the switch to phonetic writing? Probably not, but Egypt did in fact decline from world leadership, and the hieroglyphics used by Egyptian scribes were to become unintelligible for thousands of years until Napoleon's army found the Rosetta Stone. But we are ahead of our story. At the time when Greece's glory was dimming, intellectualism returned to Egypt in a big way, the result of a gift of a city from a Greek.

Alexander the Great entered Egypt in 332 B.C. He was welcomed and was soon ensconced in the capital at Memphis. Early in 331 B.C., he traveled to the Nile delta's edge, where he selected a site by the sea for a new city, to be named Alexandria. The young Greek conqueror marked out where the temples and meeting places would be, and he set the perimeter for the new city's walls.[10] The building of the new city commenced, and soon Alexander moved on: first swinging west into Egypt, then back through Memphis, and east from there to conquer across the Middle East and into India. He died eight years later, having never returned to the city that would soon conquer the intellectual world. Just about everything that was known would soon converge in Alexandria.

It was certainly no fool who had this stroke of genius: found a library at Alexandria in which to collect everything that was known, so it would not be lost and could be used by scholars from everywhere. The library began during the rule of Ptolemy I Soter, who became governor of Egypt in 323 B.C. and king in 305 B.C. The library may have been Ptolemy's idea. It served as a focal point where knowledge converged for nearly a thousand years.

The library of Alexandria teaches us the power of the idea of convergence, an important feature of the Grand Idea about to take hold of our own global intellectual resources. Once the central library was established in the Nile port city, it captured the imagination of knowledge lovers throughout the Mediterranean world and beyond. The timing was perfect for convergence because the glory of Greece scholarship was slipping, and at the same time the Roman Empire was beginning to connect the Mediterranean world by sea routes and the rest of the known world by spokes of roads into Europe, Asia, and Africa. People could travel more easily at the height of the Roman Empire than they could until the nineteenth century. The idea of the library of Alexandria was to copy all existing books. Where these works were in languages other than Greek, they were to be translated and then copied. Scholars were welcomed to take up residence in Alexandria. Thousands upon thousand of books, in the form of hand-copied scrolls, piled up in the library. Among the works translated was Hebrew scripture for use by Greek-speaking Jews:

> Jewish legend says the 72 scholars, under the sponsorship of Ptolemy Philadelphus (c. 250 BC), were brought together on the island of Pharos, near Alexandria, where they produced a Greek translation of the [Old Testament] in 72 days. From this tradition the Latin word for 70, "Septuagint," became the name attached to the translation. . . . Behind the legend lies the probability that at least the Torah (the five books of Moses) was translated into Greek c. 250 BC for the use of Greek-speaking Jews of Alexandria.[11]

As this passage illustrates, there is some uncertainty about the historical facts of the library at Alexandria. My research has uncovered little about the fate of the library that is verifiable. But that only reinforces my point: the enduring power of the library was not its effectiveness in preserving written literature, but the power of the idea of doing so. Although a lot of books were undoubtedly copied and retained, the main stories that people have been telling each other for centuries are about the fires, and these fire stories still make us wince. The great convergence project burned up over and over. Julius Caesar is blamed for one big fire, although he may not deserve it. Religious diversity, animosity, and unrest led to other conflagrations that destroyed scrolls from time to time over the centuries of the Roman Empire's decline. The rumor persists that the Arabs burned the last of the scrolls to heat the old buildings from the library when they took control of Alexandria in the seventh century, but it is not true, according to Professor Bernard Lewis of Princeton University, who also debunks another legend about Alexandria:

> A story common in many books tells us that after the Arab occupation of Alexandria the Caliph ordered the destruction of the great library of that city on the grounds that if the books contained what was in the Quran they were unnecessary, whereas if they did not they were impious. Critical scholarship has shown the story to be completely unfounded. None of the early chronicles, not even the Christian ones, make any reference to this tale, which is first mentioned in the thirteenth century.[12]

As things turned out, it was the Arabs, not the library, that ended up preserving classical books. The Arab culture absorbed and transmitted many of the good ideas of the ancient West into premodern times. Islam attached religious importance to knowledge, and that importance energized scholarship and motivated them to translate books into Arabic, not to burn them.

The library of Alexandria is a persistent vision because of the grandness of the idea of bringing all knowledge together. The thought that this very good idea was tried and failed bothers us. We want to blame people for setting fires. The library did set loose the idea of libraries, and this was copied by other cities during the heyday of scholarship at Alexandria and in the centuries that followed. The Web site of the New York Public Library explains:

The origins of this remarkable institution date back to the time when New York was emerging as one of the world's most important cities. By the second half of the 19th century, New York had already surpassed Paris in population and was quickly catching up with London, then the world's most populous city. Fortunately, this burgeoning and somewhat brash metropolis counted among its citizens men who foresaw that if New York was indeed to become one of the world's great centers of urban culture, it must also have a great library.[13]

The New Yorkers who caught the vision of the Ptolemys were John Jacob Astor, James Lenox, Samuel J. Tilden, John Bigelow, and John Shaw Billings. But by the nineteenth century, when the large library in New York was collected, the concept was great yet did not measure up to Ptolemy's vision. The grand idea of the library of Alexandria had been to have copies of all of the world's books in one place so that anyone from anywhere could come and study them.

The fabled fires of the library of Alexandria are fueled in our minds by the frustration of convergence without divergence. It is not enough to bring all knowledge to a single place, for it perishes from its own isolation. All knowledge must be accessible for ideas to be used and to grow. When the printing press came along, convergence became localized, and ideas were soon spread to every corner of the earth. The printing press could make enough copies for everyone everywhere. Printing was the dominant medium, and divergence was king.

The sculptor Donatello and Johannes Gutenberg, who invented the printing press, lived in the early fifteenth century, when the Renaissance turned the creative spirit loose in the European world. Ideas, old and new, were everywhere, and once the presses began to turn out books, the pace of printing began an acceleration that has seldom abated over five centuries.

While Gutenberg was printing Bibles, the Portuguese were exploring the west coast of Africa, and by the end of the fifteenth century, European ships had reached India and the Americas. The known world spread out from the West, and the isolation of East from West was ending. Divergence of ideas was in full sway. There were pockets of convergence, such as Amsterdam in the days of Rembrandt and London at the height of the British Empire. But not until the new devices of mass media invented in the twentieth century could anyone find out what someone was thinking about in a distant location without reading about it in a letter or book. Books were written and printed in every part of the world, in dozens of languages. Some of them were distributed broadly, but many were not. The notion of all ideas being in one place had gone up in smoke at Alexandria.

The Industrial Revolution brought people closer together through improvements in transportation, with steam engines supplementing sails on watercraft, railroads crossing countries and continents, automobiles putting people on wheels, and airplanes letting people fly. Other inventions created mass media for speeding and broadcasting ideas. Telegraph and ocean cables provided a simple way to send a code through an electric wire. The keys tapped on and off, sending starts and stops of currents that were detected by a distant receiver, where the message was decoded. Photography became a medium for recording images from reality and printing them on metal or paper. Telephones enabled voices to join dots and dashes on the wires, and radio let them ride the waves of radiant frequencies. The illusion of movement was projected as light using multiple photographs, and cinema was born. Sound was etched into wax and replicated in vibrating speakers. Color found its way into photographic emulsion, and sound tracks were recorded next to the images on movie films. Printing made great innovations in lithography, but it still relied on the movable and hot type of letterpress and Linotype to create original text images. Television brought pictures to join the sounds in the wireless world of electromagnetic radiation. Magnetic tape was developed to capture sound waves and then video. Coaxial cables were laid in trenches to connect television networks over long distances.

At least as astounding as the progress in transportation and communication over the last two hundred years is what has been learned about human history. The Rosetta Stone is a familiar story: how it was found in Egypt by Napoleon's soldiers in 1799 and soon deciphered, making it possible for scholars once again to read Egyptian hieroglyphics. But other decipherment breakthroughs are less well known. Cyrus H. Gordon has described

> the story of how forgotten scripts were deciphered and lost languages recovered, thus adding two thousand years to the documented span of Western civilization. Greece and Israel no longer stand at the dawn of history. Thanks to the decipherment of Egyptian and cuneiform, there are now fifteen centuries of recorded history in the cradle of Western culture, before the Greeks and Hebrews appeared on the scene. Moreover, the earliest inscriptions pertaining to the Hellenes and Israelites antedate the composition of the Iliad and of Genesis.[14]

Everything that is known by living scholars now includes more and more of what was known by people alive in the past. That is wonderful, and so are our greatly enhanced powers of communication over those of earlier generations. Could it have been that the ghost of Ptolemy I Soter attended the great celebrations at the pyramids by the Nile as the clocks signaled the arrival of the year 2000? If he had access that night to television, it might have seemed to him the apex of possible convergence and divergence. The whole world was watching Egypt at that moment, and as the midnight beginning of the year moved around Earth, he could watch what seemed like the whole world through his television screen. But Ptolemy would not find a fulfillment of his vision of the library at Alexandria. Y2K was a great party night, but has media become mainly hype?

NOTES

1. Walter L. Friedrich, *Fire in the Sea* (New York: Cambridge University Press, 2000), appendix 1, 209.

2. Gordon M. Shepherd, *Neurobiology,* 3d ed. (New York: Oxford University Press, 1994), 125.

3. Michael H. Brown, *The Search for Eve* (New York: Harper and Row, 1990), 10.

4. "The Human Family Tree: 10 Adams and 18 Eves," *New York Times*, 2 May 2000, Science Times.

5. David Firestone, "Anonymous Louisiana Slaves Regain Identity," *New York Times*, 30 July 2000.

6. Genesis 11:1–9.

7. Herodotus, *The Histories,* Book 6, trans. George Rawlison <http://classics.mit. edu/Herodotus/history.sum.html>, [accessed 3 August, 2000].

8. Edith Hamilton, *The Echo of Greece* (New York: W. W. Norton, 1957), 17.

9. Hamilton, 9–10.

10. Robin Lane Fox, *The Search for Alexander* (Boston: Little, Brown, 1980), 195.

11. *The New International Version Study Bible* (Grand Rapids, Mich.: Zondervan Publishing House, 1985), 1431–32.

12. Bernard Lewis, *The Arabs in History* (New York: Oxford University Press, 1993), 53.

13. New York Public Library Web page, New York Public Library <http://www.nypl. org/admin/pro/history.html>, 5 May 1996 [accessed 3 August 2000].

14. Cyrus H. Gordon, *Forgotten Scripts* (New York: Basic, 1982), xvi.

III

THE GREAT CHANGE

It must have taken quite a while before thinking people in Europe caught on to what was really out there as explorers began coming back from voyages west to take a look at the Americas. Informed people would understand that when Vasco da Gama made it all the way around Africa, he was trying to get to the China reported by Marco Polo and already accessible by land via the Silk Road. But another half of the world? A New Spain? A New France? A New England? The most powerful nation in human history will form over there? Really?

The Great Change now under way is even bigger because what will be new is how very, very much we will be able to know.

4

Digital Soup

Imagine, if you will, a large bowl into which you throw your books, your letters and notes, your music collection, your radio and television set, your telephone and fax, and all of your pictures of family and friends. Toss in the Rosetta Stone too. You then pour a magic, sparkling substance over everything in the bowl and stir. Soon the contents mix into a smooth and uniform single substance. Turn a knob on the side of a bowl, and your music plays. Click a nearby switch, and you are watching your favorite television show. An interactive family album icon is offered on your bowlside control panel. Your library is accessible through a multi-indexed catalog. A viewer lets you see the words etched on the Rosetta in the three original languages and in English. An Internet button takes you into the World Wide Web.

The buttons here are fanciful, but the soup is a fact of life today. Few people outside the technical arena seem to understand that such a world already exists, much less that it has liberated us from scribal slavery to a dawning age of thinking prowess. Because the machine handles the transmission details, we can think the thoughts. Computer scientist Daniel Hillis explains:

> Naming two signals in computer logic 0 and 1 is an example of functional abstraction. It lets us manipulate information without worrying about the details of its underlying representation. Once we figure out how to accomplish a given function, we can put the mechanism inside a "black box" or a "building block" and stop thinking about it. The function embodied by the building block can be used over and over, without reference to the details of what's inside.[1]

Before information can be processed through a black box of this sort, it has to be coded in language the machine can understand. Digitizing information reduces it to a sequence of zeros and ones that have become the granular common denominator for words, sounds, images, computer codes, for any and every form of information conceivable. Numbers and letters were among the first representations of knowledge to be assigned digital or binary codes. A is represented by 01000001, B is 01000011, and C is 0100 0011. Colors are created on-screen by codes of zeros and ones that instruct pixels to assume specific intensities related to their hues. Whether for the simplest or the most complex operations, a computer understands only zeros and ones.

The sequence of zeros and ones that represent information can be chopped up into packets that are tagged, sent somewhere along with other packets, and reassembled at a distant location. Words, sounds, and images can be transformed (digitized) off of their paper, vinyl, and emulsions into zeros and ones, sent somewhere else, and then put back onto paper, wax (compact discs [CDs] are better), and photographic print grounds.

What is known and who knows it are not to be confused with how stuff is processed in the digital world. The Great Change into the digital soup is the fact that everything is communicated in the same code. Analog and other older methods required different methods of communication for different types of media. When you look at a snapshot printed from negative film, you hold in your hand an analog device communicating an image that your brain constructs in your head. When you look at the same picture on your monitor screen, you are viewing a digitally communicated display from which your brain constructs an image in your head. In predigital times, different kinds of information were communicated on different kinds of analog devices, including visual images on film, sound on wax (and later plastic) disks, and words on printed pages (letterpress, lithography, rotogravure). Visual images, sound, words, and virtually all other representations of human ideas can now be morphed into the digital soup, communicated, and then interfaced so that the mind can reconstruct them. In the digital soup, there are just two things: zeros and ones.

Analog devices are easier to grasp intuitively than the digital ones. Take color photography. In 1935, Eastman Kodak introduced Kodachrome film. For the first time the multilayer principle was employed successfully, leading to rapid advancement in color photography. Multilayer film makes separate records of red, green, and blue light reflected from a photographic subject onto three emulsions, each of which responds to one of the three primary colors. The trick was to put all three emulsions onto one piece of photographic paper, serving as a ground. The principle of three emulsions had been tried before, using three separate grounds, which led to fuzziness in moving subjects. Another approach, that cost too much, had been using optical setups that split the light using prisms into three colors before they reached the film. Kodachrome perfected a medium that you could hold in your hand and look at as a picture, seeing a snapshot that was analogous to the real thing. Baby Sue in the photograph looked like the real Baby Sue, in color!

Another extremely popular analog medium that became popular in the early twentieth century was the phonograph. Big round platters were spun around contained grooves, which were followed by a needle. The grooves were cut with wiggles and bumps that recorded the vibrations of a piece of music. The needle tracked the wiggles and bumps, and they were converted into analogous waves going over wires into a speaker that vibrated to cause the human eardrum to respond by sending a music signal to the brain. When Al Jolson sang at the recording studio, the grooves he cut were capable of causing a sound analogous to his voice to sing, "When the red, red robin comes bob, bob, bobbin' along. . . ."

It is not intuitive to think of Baby Sue's smile and Jolson's robin reduced to the form of zeros and ones. Yet they can be, and when they are it is possible for them to be communicated through the same information pipe: Baby Sue's image and Al Jolson's voice squirt through the glass pipe as sequences of zeros and ones. What happens is based on the same concept as Morse code. When telegraph wires reached across the American continent in 1869, it was stunningly new that the same message could be sent to people on both seacoasts at the same time. To do so by telegraph required reducing information to a simple code of dots and dashes. Because somebody at each end of the wire knew the same code, the sender could reduce the meaning of the message to the rules of the code, and the receiver could reconstruct the meaning from the code at the other end. It was still tap, tap, tap, whether what was transmitted was election news or a telegram from Cousin Bessie.

To realize the simplicity here, do not wander off into wondering how bits and bytes are used to multiply the messages generated by selecting either one or zero (on or off) at the granular level of the process. The key is: one soup, one pipe. Remember, this is about communicating everything, not about the essence of the things communicated. Beethoven's symphonies, Rembrandt's self-portraits, Baby Sue's picture, the Bible, the Koran, the works of Shakespeare, your banking records—anything that can be known is reducible to zeros and ones. Like the telegraph, the material to be sent is coded (digitized) by the sender and reconstituted into an apprehensible interface for the receiver.

There is no need to think about the digital soup in a complicated way. Enjoy, instead, its elegance. The digital code was in fact created as the simplest way to construct computers. Digitization is the daughter of deduction, where there is only right and wrong.

> Socrates is a man.
> All men are mortal.
> Socrates is mortal.

Any gate on a computer chip can only be open or shut. The idea is that if there were a gate open indicating that Socrates is a man, and an adjacent gate open indicating that all men are mortal, the next gate on the logic tree, querying the mortal state of Socrates, would open.

But computers do not use the meaning of words, they just recognize sequences of zeros and ones. What is going on is a little bit like the fact that the complexities of our bodies are devised from just a few kinds of atoms. By processes far more complicated than what any existing computer could handle, the coding of our DNA and ultimately into the working combination that is our body. Genetic information that accomplishes this comes in combinations of four units called A, G, C, and T; our genome uses a four-letter code instead of the two-option code we use in computers. The DNA function for computers is the programming done by humans to use the zeros and ones to send signals for myriad purposes. The technical people in such tremendous demand at such high salaries today do this work.

Programmers write code that ultimately consists of sequences of zeros and ones. A very human habit explains why such sequences are known as digital rather than the more appropriate term binary, which suggests just two states — one/zero, on/off, open/shut — that are the reality of what we call the digital world. In Middle English, *digitus* meant finger, derived from Greek *deiknynai,* which meant to show. People seem always to have had the habit of showing numbers with their fingers — check it out with any three-year-old. The binary numbers on the IBM cards used in the heyday of mainframe computers could be read visually. Each numeral, 0,1,2,3,4,5,6,7,8, and 9, had been assigned a binary code. At set locations on the IBM cards the numbers were coded by punching a hole or not punching a hole at each possible location. A hole sent a zero to the computer and no hole sent a one. In the early days of computing those working with the code would tend to hold up a sequence of fingers to represent the binary numbers, and the name digital caught on for numbers represented by some fingers up and others down.

The computer world rests upon an elegant simplicity: there are always just two options. The binary principle, now known as digital, operates computers by opening gates or leaving them closed, and by leaving sequences of zeros and ones in magnetic memory. Digital information can be hard-coded onto CDs, where the surface is etched with a pattern of thousands upon thousands of minute locations that are either holes or not holes. The laser light beam that scans the CD sends a signal of on/off sequences that the audio receiver translates into words, sounds, and images.

The digital soup can contain ideas that have been represented in many types of media because it is a bowl full of code. The soup and the bowl are not media. Digital media are constructed to read the code. The zeros and ones can come down a wire, be etched onto a CD, and travel through transistors, carrying with it all in the same code: music, sound, images, and everything that was ever known.

We are drowning in digital hype about three major phenomena it has generated: technology, communication, and business. There has been little focus so far on a fourth area, which I think is the big one: ideas.

Many of the brightest people of our time have become fascinated with digital technology and have used it to move the world from the industrial age into the age of technology. There are excellent books galore from which to learn the history, challenges, and prospects issuing from the now ubiquitous zeros and ones that are the lifeblood of the technical world of today and tomorrow.

Communication is morphing at warp speed into the digital ubiquity. Telephone wires have turned to glass, and satellites bounce news, phone calls, and instructions to guidance systems (to mention a few things) from any here to any there. The Internet is connecting millions of new people each month. The U.S. Post Office wants to give everyone an e-mail address. Entire countries are forgetting about telephone systems and relying on wireless cell phones. All of this is in the news every day, and there are many excellent books on the subject.

Business has gone digital big time! The largest corporations, mergers, and salaries go to the digital players. E-commerce and business-to-business operations loom on the horizon as even small Main Street businesses are getting Web sites. Intranets have become the communication mainstays of enterprises in both private and public sectors. Even the stock exchanges are supplemented by after-hours trading conducted over the Internet. Information about digital business is stacked up on newsstands and in bookstores.

Ideas in digital form will cause the greatest change and the most significant human advancement of these four phenomena spooned from the digital soup. The remainder of this book tells you why and how this will happen. We do not have to elaborate how the technology works, or the details of the communication, nor the business models. The first phase of the Great Change has been the digitizing of ideas, and we are far down that road.

The next phase of the Great Change is the emergence of hyperwebs; in retrospect, they were inevitable once the digital soup was served. It used to be that paper was necessary for writing, checkbooks for bank accounts, and index cards for mailing lists. By the 1980s lots of people had personal computers on which they could handle all of these things with programs that ran zeros and ones through the gates on the chips of their motherboards. Floppy disks had to go in and out because memory was limited. Full unrestrictedness and dimensionlessness had not yet been achieved. But hyperwebs had been born.

NOTES

1. W. Daniel Hillis, *The Pattern on the Stone* (New York: Basic, 1998), 18–19.

5

Hyperwebs

In earlier chapters I mention trees in several contexts. I do this in order to create a foil against which to contrast hyperwebs. We like to use treelike outlines to organize our thoughts. Using hyperwebs to structure ideas is the same kind of thing, but the hyperwebs provide far superior organization than trees do. *Hyper* means that anything can connect to anything, going in any and every direction. Hyperwebs are more complex than trees. They better reflect the way we think. They more deeply follow the pattern of the nature of nature. A tree gives a fine pattern for a natural tree, with everything branching out, but as what we know about nature deepens, a tree is proving a failure for realities such as the relations of species. As we shall see, even the tree of life is turning out to be a web.

Out of our new digital world arise hyperwebs. They place no limits on what can be connected to what, and they can be explored in a nonlinear way. Hyperwebs allow us to move to a powerful and wonderful new structural reflection of ideas outside of the mind. If that sounds hard to understand, it is only because hyperwebs are new, not because they are complicated. Simply put: we now have a new medium that mimics the interconnectedness of thought. We are able to use this medium to manipulate ideas individually as students, in groups as teachers, and across the globe on the Internet. Soon the Grand Idea will shift into existence as a new paradigm accessible to all.

Using a tree to reflect thought is working from the trunk to the leaves or from the leaves to the trunk. Stephen Jay Gould has observed that "like bureaucracy, knowledge has an inexorable tendency to ramify as it grows."[1] To *ramify* is to *branch*; *ramus* means *branch* in Latin. But just because branching is involved, it is superficial to assume that ideas grow on trees. Ideas grow in human minds. Although the workings of the human mind remain among the great puzzles to be solved, the workings of ideas can be seen in fascinating new ways as they cascade into digital media. Ideas branch and ramify before us with new speed, clarity, and richness. The forms that emerge are hyperwebs, not trees.

In discussing the mirrors we use for ideas, we looked at how the abstract structure of a tree is a very limited way to organize what we are thinking. The NBA Store on Fifth Avenue in Manhattan uses a tree to display the play-offs in its window. Jerseys for each of the teams are mounted on cardboard and arranged up the two sides of the window as the preliminary rounds begin. As teams advance, duplicates of their jerseys are moved toward the center, again paired as opponents in each game of the rounds. When the championship has been won, a jersey of the winning team is placed in the center, with the play-off games now branching out from both sides. The tree diagram organizes the games in logical order in the simplest manner. It gives no details. It gives no indication of how Michael Jordan's retirement affected Chicago's chances as compared to other years. We know that in a very complicated reality what put the winning jersey in the middle is a whole lot of things, little and big, that built up to the climax.

Outlining things—organizing them as they branch out—is very useful. Trial lawyers do it to build their cases. As in competitive debate, trial lawyers are going for a deductive sort of proof like the Socrates syllogism. There are two very different sides in a trial. On one side, the accused is innocent until proven guilty. Although juries are impressed by a logical case by the defense, proof of innocence is not required. On the other side, a logical case must be made to prove guilt, and a logical outline is a very helpful tool in this process:

> The murderer stole the red necklace.
> Harry was found with the red necklace.
> Harry is the murderer.

The trial lawyer tries to use deductive logic to make his case as certainly true as the processes in a computer where the gates can only be open or shut. But it is not easy to do in a courtroom. The rules of deductive logic require that the first two statements of a syllogism be proved before the conclusion can be true. Inductive proof has to be brought in: eyewitness accounts, circumstantial evidence, and the like are necessary to support the lawyer's summation of having proved the defendant's guilt.

Logical outlines and syllogisms are treelike in structure because they branch down from premises to prove central conclusions. They are highly directional. Are trees false tools? Of course not. For one thing, if they were, they would not work in computers. Are they then false tools for thinking? No, in fact they are useful tools when they apply well to the topic, but they are often superficial and limited. Most important to understand is that the treelike outlines are tools we apply to reality—they are not reality itself. We seldom find a real tree structure embedded in nature, because most of nature is weblike. Trees are not reality, and they do not reflect much of the richness of human thinking. Tools are *heuristic*: "involving or serving as an aid to learning, discovery, or problem-solving by experiment and esp. trial-and-error methods."[2] Just as mathematics is a human invention, so are phyla. As we quoted the biologists earlier: *only the species is specific.*[3]

Still, organizing things by classifications—breaking them out into smaller and smaller branches of a big class—is something we are very used to doing. Putting stuff into hyperwebs is a big improvement, as we shall see. Ernst Mayr has defined classification in these words:

> In daily life, one can deal with a large number of very different items only by classifying them. Classifications are used for the ordering of tools, drugs, and art objects, as well as for theories, concepts, and ideas. When we classify, we group objects into classes according to their shared attributes. A class, then, is an assemblage of entities that are similar and related to one another.[4]

What if the relationships in the real world can be formed in zillions of ways, and we can think up those relationships in dozens of ways—but we have been pretty much stuck up to now with mirroring these relationships with just a few structural principles that can be coped with using paper and other physical media? I believe that is the case, and that the virtual environment of computers releases us from physical limitations.

A good example of physical limitations to organizing ideas is how libraries used to be cataloged. Reference rooms had two sets of little wooden drawers filled with cards arranged in alphabetical order. You could use one set to look up books by author and the other set to look up books by title. When you selected a book, there would be a number on the card telling you how the book was classified. Books would be arranged on the shelves according to the numbers assigned to them by the classification system. This system was very effective spacewise because a book could have a single number assigning it to a shelf while having two different ways to find it in the catalog. There were two top-down classification systems dictating how the books were categorized and where the librarians put them. There were two trees, and the numbering system could have been displayed on the flat plane of the NBA Store window; it would take the same form as the jerseys. We would have imposed an organizational mirror on a complex reality. Because of computers, of course, libraries are now breaking free from the limited linearity of hard-copy card files.

Many years ago, my father tried to beat the card file limitations by using a system called McBee Cards. A pioneer orthopaedic surgeon, Dad published over a hundred original papers in his lifetime, and twenty-five years after it was first published, his article on hip replacement was republished as the "classic" by a national orthopaedic association. He practiced medicine during the time of great progress in orthopaedics when, from the late 1930s to the late 1950s, osteomyelitis and spinal tuberculosis had been cured and polio prevented with vaccines. Nailing broken hips was perfected and then superseded by prosthetic hip replacements. My father and several partners accumulated thousands of patient records.

Dad was determined to mine a lot of scientific data out of the records, but it was not easy in those days. The McBee Cards were about three by seven inches, and lines were provided to write the name of the subject of the card, the date of treatment, and other identifying information. The cards had holes punched all the way around the edges, and each hole had a number. Dad set up a system where a patient's name, age, and a few other details were written on the card. He made a list of diagnoses and assigned a number to each. Dislocated shoulder might be 18, while a cracked patella might be 38. The system worked by using a handheld clipper to cut along the edge so that a hole was changed into a v-shaped slot: if the patient had had a dislocated shoulder, hole 18 became a slot, and so forth. After all the cards were clipped, they were put into a rack where they were neat and even. A needle tool resembling an ice pick was then run through, say, the location of hole 18. You would then lift the cards with the needle, shake carefully, and all the dislocated shoulder cards would drop out. Next, if you needled through the 38s, you would have a stack of patients who had cracked patellas. By comparing them, you might find a pattern, perhaps of muscle weakness contributing to both kinds of injuries.

Primitive as digging out those comparisons with a slotted-card method seems now, it was innovative at the time because it provided a way to mine valuable comparisons from storerooms full of bulky files. Those comparisons were medically important. I can remember well my grandmother's cavernous basement where rows and rows of huge, square, manila-colored envelopes held the x-ray images and treatment details of three decades, in chronological order. Dad grasped in his mind the value of hyperwebs and was able to use McBee Cards to access data from the shelves. He managed to work from the inside out: from the granular level of all the diagnoses on the shelves, up to comparisons among them, and then to some general observations. He knew that orthopaedic ideas are not best organized in chronological or alphabetical order, and that the relationship among diagnoses could not be outlined on a tree. Research in the biological sciences could not be constructed like a lawyer's brief.

How is reality organized? The digital soup has made possible a new reflective tool with which to capture the weblike nature of much of the world out there. Duke University biology professor Steven Vogel's book, *Cats' Paws and Catapults,* compares the "Mechanical Worlds of Nature and People." Among the many interesting comparisons he makes is this one:

> Nature builds upward from molecules and cells, while we usually don't. Some things, though, are more easily made that way. For instance, you hook together in specific sequences the different amino acids that form your proteins as directed by your genetic code, not by brewing up a batch of identical little molecules and making them stick to each other in random order. You also make composites like bone by synthesizing and positioning the various components and letting the product solidify.[5]

In the structure of our brains, there is dazzling complexity from the level of genes, up to macromolecules in synapses, to the astonishing multitude of synaptic variations, to microcircuits of abounding diversity, to nerve cells of many types, to local circuits doing myriad jobs, to systems distributed through the brain, to behaviors resulting from the function of all the levels of structure.[6] The treelike branching of nerve endings gives us a clue to hyperwebs. The branches of the neurons are called *dendrites*, from a root word *dendron*, which means *tree* in Greek. Images of dendrites look just like trees, but they do something that trees cannot do. A tree is like a plumbing system in which the pipes get smaller in one direction and larger in the other direction. You pour the water into the main pipe at the city reservoir, and it spreads out through smaller and smaller pipes until it flows out of the system into your sink. The brain, however, has a fundamental flexibility absent from such a water system: at just about any point, what is flowing can be mixed with stuff flowing into and out of other parts of the system. You would make a big mistake if you connected the water coming into your sink to the main sewer in the street outside your house, even if you could imagine a way to do that. There is no possibility of feedback in a tree. Once a branch has left the trunk it cannot nourish branches that left the trunk at other places.

To anticipate the importance of hyperwebs on a grand scale, note that the Internet is a hyperweb, not a tree. There is not even a trunk. Every place there is a connection to the Internet can be connected to every other place there is a connection to the Internet. Connections are routed through hubs and nodes, but there is no limit to what can be connected to what, and exploring the Internet is done nonlinearly. But the World Wide Web does not connect ideas, it connects locations.

The suspended sphere of the new Hayden Planetarium in New York City hangs to the north of the American Museum of Natural History, in the park where the giant balloons are inflated for the annual Macy's Thanksgiving Day Parade. Within the glass box surrounding the uplifted ball of the theater, the Cullman Hall of the Universe spreads across the lower floor, offering exhibits of the latest knowledge of the cosmos. The Cosmic Horizon legend explains: "Although we are at the center of our cosmic horizon, the universe has neither a center nor an edge. Every point in space is at the center of its own cosmic horizon. Like a ship at sea, we float in a vast cosmic ocean, unable to see its true extent."

A gorgeous postcard with a computer-generated image of current understanding of the structure of the Observable Universe is published by the planetarium. The card's legend says: "This rendering of the Observable Universe shows a tangled web of superclusters of galaxies, each of which contains billions of suns. The Milky Way Galaxy is one of several thousand galaxies in the Virgo Supercluster, which is one of the brightest spots pictured."

As I said early on, ideas come into being by connecting things. Up until the flowering of digital technologies, our only effective tangible mirror for reflecting complex connections in our minds was art. Of course, language has always spoken to the theater of the mind, allowing us to listen to or read its linear recitation, and then tie things together in nonlinear ways in our thinking: we could enjoy flashbacks that were out of sequence in a story, and relate the book we read last year to material now being studied.

With art, we are able to reflect complex relationships in nature and from our minds. Most often the dimensionless relationships that give deeper meaning to painting are submerged in subject matter and pictorial representation, but in good art they are always there. A genius who enjoyed cognitive art—thinking that is depicted—was Paul Klee. His paintings resonate with visual relationships. Wander, for example, through his 1934 painting "Blossoming": the hot orange below the center echoes the large cool orange receding up to the left, and that backward movement is felt in the cool orange anchoring the upper center and darkly shadowed to the right near the edge. The yellows and yellow-greens bounce in and out, and everything is linked to everything else by its squareness. I believe the beauty we experience from art derives largely from our ineffable understanding of the richness of relationships unconfined to linearity. These relationships mirror the capacity of our mind to connect scraps of thought into a hyperweb that becomes an idea.

Digital technologies have given us a radically new heuristic tool for organizing anything, and this tool takes a large step beyond classification toward a more accurate and complex mirror of both reality and of how we think. We hope that how we think does a useful job of mirroring reality. How exciting it would be if a medium came along into which we could store and from which we could interface the reality we construct in our minds. Ideas are webs because that is what it takes to grasp reality. The new digital medium grasps this webness, and that is a very big deal.

Certainly a tree is a useful heuristic tool, and nothing better will come along to reflect the organization of the NBA play-offs. But the hyperweb tool is far more versatile because it can reflect unlimited relationships in unlimited dimensions. There is no way to do that on paper, because paper is a two-dimensional plane. The digital soup, however, works splendidly. In the digital soup, as in nature, little things coalesce to form bigger things, and these, in turn, establish relationships with other things. In the digital soup, at any stage for anything in the system, its substance is sequences of zeros and ones. The result is frictionless movement through the hyperweb: things do not have to be transformed into sound waves or color information while they are in the hyperweb. Only when they exit the system do they become intelligible to humans by being sent to speakers or displayed as pixels.

One might think that richness and complexity would be lost by reducing things to just two states, one or zero, but the opposite is the case. The greatest known richness grows upward from simpler things. You and I began with the convergence of the DNA from two cells, each containing information stored in just four different code units—just two more than the one and zero digital code. But do not expect anything more complicated to grow out of the digital soup except our stunning new way to send information from one place to another. Hyperwebs exploit this to present material in unlimited relationships. The wonder of this was glimpsed by a few early visionaries, as is discussed in the next two chapters.

The converging and diverging power of the soup is made possible because everything has been reduced to the same code and thus can be moved around and decoded somewhere else. Using the quantum world as a metaphor, meaningful content of all sorts has morphed into energy to allow it to move with all other content through a system of related points: a hyperweb. The amount of energy has no theoretical limit in the digital arena, and the number of possible dimensions that can be created is unlimited as well. Before we examine large-scale hyperwebs in cyberspace, it is appropriate to recount the origins of hyperwebs in mirroring ideas—including the beginning of the Great Change in education.

NOTES

1. Stephen Jay Gould, foreword to *Five Kingdoms*, by Lynn Margulis and V. Schwartz, (New York: Freeman,1998), xi.
2. *Merriam-Webster's Collegiate Dictionary,* 10th ed., 1997.
3. Margulis and Schwartz, *Five Kingdoms*, xvii.
4. Ernst Mayr, *This Is Biology* (Cambridge: Harvard University Press, 1997), 125.
5. Steven Vogel, *Cats' Paws and Catapults* (New York: W. W. Norton, 1998), 280.
6. Gordon M. Shepherd, *Neurobiology* (New York: Oxford University Press, 1994), 6.

6

Hypermirrors

Could it be that few people understand what computers are because they are called *computers*? The name is almost as opaque as *digital* is for *binary*. Today *Merriam-Webster's* has the following definitions of computers, with dates when the words were coined:

> The root of the word *computer* (1616) is *computare*, the Latin word for count.
> *Computer* (1646) is one that computes . . . [and] a programmable electronic device that can store, retrieve, and process data.
> Computerize (1957) means to carry out, control, or produce by means of a computer.[1]

The 1966 edition of *Webster's* does not yet have the portion of the definition of *computer* above, but gives these definitions for the word:

> One who computes: as **a**: a calculator esp. designed for the solution of complex mathematical problems; specif : an automatic electronic machine for performing simple and complex calculations **b**: any of several devices for making rapid calculations in navigation or gunnery . . . **c**: a person who calculates (as latitudes, longitudes, and areas) for map making.[2]

Just as the word *digit*, meaning *finger*, came along in the earliest phases of binary development, the word meaning *count* stuck because computers first showed off their prowess by crunching numbers. They mirrored adding machines and calculators in an awesome new medium. As radically new machines have risen from the digital soup and the hyperwebs it creates, calling them counting machines has become inadequate. Of course, at the lowest plane of function, computers are still all about numbers. In this realm, though, the numbers are not counted or added or subtracted or otherwise used in calculations. The numbers are all zeros and ones. They stream through chips, opening and not opening gates, computing logic, not numbers. The first ideas computed in this manner were arithmetic ones: sums, multiplication results, and the solutions to numerical equations. Arithmetic was just the beginning. The zeros and ones are now used to compute a staggering spectrum of human ideas and to mirror the results in increasingly efficacious and beautiful interfaces.

Programming a computer is giving it instructions for opening or closing gates in sequences that cause logical outcomes. In the beginning, the mainframe computers that filled large rooms could only crunch numbers, but they could process vast amounts of mathematical tasks in very short times, and they soon rescued legion bookkeepers from tedium, much as the steam shovel had done for ditchdiggers using picks and shovels a generation before. (As I typed the last sentence into my word processing program, the spell check rejected *ditchdigger*, a word that does appear in my 1966 dictionary. Times do change: if you were born less than fifty years ago, you probably have never seen a row of men swinging picks in tandem to dig a ditch in the ground.)

The number-crunching talents of computers quickly began to transform science and accounting. Computers had become hypermirrors of the mathematical processes of the human mind. Computers do not think, but they allow us to insert our thinking rules into their chips that then process information we provide. In the past half-century, many of our most intelligent people have become captivated by the challenge of programming the machines. In recent years entire industries have been transformed by what the machines have been taught to do. The Grand Idea will soon become the most beautiful hypermirror of all. But we get ahead of the story. Next, we look at some of the major steps—hypermirrors brought online for big jobs that people used to do with their minds without computers.

When word processing was becoming practical, I was typing a book for an author. Once I realized that with a computer I would never have to type anything more than once, I pleaded for a machine. The author was generous, and I obtained my first personal computer. How does a machine that crunches numbers deal with letters? Once again, the principle is simple: each letter and all the other characters on the keyboard are assigned a unique code of zeros and ones. Type an *o*, and the o code of zeros and ones goes into the machine. Type a *k*, and the k code goes in. Hit the spacebar, and the code for a space goes in. The word processing program has rules different from the number calculation programs. The powerful underlying concept is known as *strings*. The rule is that when I type a quotation mark at the beginning of a sequence of words, and a second quotation mark at the end of my string, the computer is able to work with that string of words as a whole. You do not see the quotation marks at the beginning and ends of strings on the monitor screen anymore, but they are there virtually for the machine to define the string. Thus I can mark ("highlight" is the current parlance) a string, cut it out of a paragraph, and then paste it into a paragraph somewhere else in my text. *Hyper* implies that there is no limit to what can be connected to what. The mind can connect ideas without limit. Word processing mirrored that hyperpower for strings of words. Now when the author moved a sentence or paragraph to a different location in the manuscript, I could cut and paste, mirroring his change of mind about where an idea belonged in the whole.

Beginning in the late 1950s, I worked for a candidate who ran three times for state office in Texas. In the first campaign, we developed a system of keeping track of his supporters by making two three-by-five index cards for each of them. One card was filed alphabetically by last name, and the other was filed alphabetically within the supporter's county of residence. By the end of the second campaign we had more than five thousand names in more than a dozen file boxes that sat on tables in the headquarters. After the election, which was a second loss for the candidate, someone added to the misery of defeat by breaking into the headquarters, dumping all of the cards on the floor, and mixing them up by throwing them around. Friends of the candidate worked for months to put the cards back into the boxes correctly.

A computer database mirrors the filing system we had for the candidate. The mirror is hyper both because the physical limitation of the boxes is gone and because every hypercard can be tagged without limit. In the case of the candidate's supporters, we would have had one card for each supporter, with fields for last name, county, and anything else we could think of—from party affiliation and campaign contributions to number of children and color of hair. (As my father used the McBee system as a hard-copy database, the needle that could select the notched card gave Dad hyperpower to sort diagnoses.) Like its talents for mathematical calculations, the computer's database abilities are mirrors of how humans think about things, but the computers are masters of quantity. It was impracticable to have more than two sets of hard-copy records for the candidate. But once computers had been programmed to sort hypercards, we could have added limitless cards and limitless ways to sort. Reflecting some of the various sortings back into political thinking is very useful. We might have raised enough money to win if we had known, perhaps, some of the comparisons a database would have yielded.

It is not enough for a computer to crunch the numbers, process words, and sort virtual cards. Human beings must be able to look in the mirror to see what has been produced, and the tools for doing that are interfaces. For a long time, monitor screens could only display numbers and letters. Many of the useful and attractive innovations that have harnessed the computer are actually advances in interfacing. The spreadsheet is an example of a very good interface idea. It is used just about universally in accounting. The simple idea is to have cells spread both horizontally and vertically across the monitor screen. Cells are assigned letters across the top and numbers down the side. The interface allows you to put numbers in any of the cells and to request the calculation of any cells you identify into a designated cell. You can add cell b4 to cell b9. You can multiply cell d9 by cell a4. All the machine does is place its calculations into a certain spot on your spreadsheet interface, instead of in a list on a plain-text screen. The interface thus visually displays nonlinear, hyperrelationships.

As images began to enter the digital environment, the monitor screen and its pixels played a major role in the interfacing. Many clever ideas and inventions mirror to our visual cortex ideas that others have sketched and scanned into digital memory. A major industry that has been totally transformed is printing. Through the first half of the twentieth century, Gutenberg's movable type was still the mainstay of printing. Lithography made printing possible from metal and paper images, but the originals from which the plates were made were hot metal type or metal type removed from racks and placed in a frame just as Gutenberg did it. The echo of this remains in software graphics and word processing programs that still offer you type sizes in points, based on the old hard type. The print shops had metal type in standard point sizes such as 24, 36, 48, and 72, just like your software. In the old days, if you wanted 29-point type, you were out of luck, because there was no type that size on the shelf. In the computer graphics world, there is no reason to have the set sizes, because somebody thought of scalable type.

Scalable type was a very good idea that solved a big problem. Letters are displayed on a monitor screen by making the little pixel dots black. A row of black dots straight up is an *l* and a circle of dots forms an o. To make a 24-point *l,* twice as many dots up are needed than for a 12-point *l.* Scalable type avoids counting the dots by describing the shape of each letter. Thus the program is told how high to make the letter, and the computer draws the shape. The computer graphics industry works in the raster world (dots) and the vector world (shapes) to give us a magnificent mirror of what we write, draw, paint, and see in our mind's eye. With publishing programs, computers began to create the pages and plates for printing complex documents, and then books.

Like a child growing up, computers went through stages in learning to process ideas. For a long time the emphasis was on skills: math and words. After a while, images were processed with increasing sophistication. Meanwhile, computers were getting faster and faster, and their memories were growing more and more vast. Floppy disks that could hold a few pages were replaced by compact discs (CDs) that could hold a few books. The computer was getting mature enough to hypermirror not only some basic human thinking processes, but its collective memory was absorbing what humans know.

Very early on, the visionary Gutenberg Project began enlisting volunteers to type books into programs that would code their text into zeros and ones. The process had begun of digitizing recorded human knowledge—a process now nearing completion, as the Grand Idea will reflect. Active science began to be practiced mainly in digital machines, with notes and experiments beginning never to find their way onto paper. One supposes the ever-growing details of the Human Genome Project have not been recorded in full printed form for a long time.

From the dawning of the digital age there have been futurists who have predicted that education would be changed by computers. Yet as the machines became indispensable for scientists, lawyers and other wordsmiths, accountants and bankers, printers and publishers, education could not or did not embrace the digital tools. An entire generation of students continued to use nondigital learning tools in school, even as their parents became dependent on computers at the workplace. Of course, the kids got into computers through games, music, and running cash registers at their jobs, but at school they wrote mostly with pencils and studied from textbooks reprinted every few years. Some of the tools so useful to their parents in the workplace did trickle down to the schools. From the earlier insistence that students learn to figure in their heads, electronic calculators gradually acquired a place in math classrooms. Word processing began to go digital in college dorms and, slowly, in the homes of well-off high school students.

To finish explaining the Great Change, and then to move on to the Grand Idea, a distinction must be made between repositioning classroom tasks and mirroring the mind. Until the Internet burst on the scene, the discussion of computers in education was almost completely about noncognitive matters. Larry Cuban wrote a book in 1986 about education's "fickle romance" with technology, focusing on film, radio, instructional television, and computers. Here is Cuban's description of how computers were used in schools in 1986:

> Teachers and administrators are the primary users. The computer's power to store, process, and retrieve information about attendance, scheduling, grades, inventories, and a host of other clerical tasks makes it ideal for administrative uses both in the principal's office and the classroom. Other classroom uses fall into the visual workbook category, with simulations, writing, and machine tutoring among the less-used options. Teaching students to program computers appears to be increasing.[3]

In 1986, computers were a lousy place to look for ideas. They had little memory and were very seldom connected to each other. The hypermirroring of the rich ideas of human knowledge by computers lay in the future. Yet there were early efforts to involve computers in learning that explored the possibilities of new ways to connect ideas. Apple's Hypercard software was used by computer gurus and visionary teachers to create rudimentary digital tutors. In 1990, Kristina Hooper, director of Apple Computer's Multimedia Lab, wrote: "Hypercard is fundamentally designed to address how people think rather than how processors might work effectively. We can now design pedagogical surrounds with tools designed to be compatible with mental activities."[4]

Malcolm Thompson, a master pioneer of hyperweb tutors and while teaching at the Dalton School, developed software lessons in science that his students used on a computer before they took the course he taught in person. Several years ago, I heard him explain that the kids did better in his course because of what they learned working through the lessons on the computer.

A computer's talent to tutor children with developmental disorders was tapped in the early days of desktop computers. Kids who seemed never to catch on could move beyond their handicaps when a computer drilled, because the machine could exercise inhuman patience and was incapable of embarrassing kids with the human nuances of frustration. In some instances Lew Robins's Everybody Can Read software did a better job of teaching than parents or teachers, and helped children for whom hope for literacy had been abandoned.[5]

Although they are often intertwined, there are two major ways computers assist learning. The first is by reflecting the ideas that are to be learned. It is to give us access to knowledge, like a book or a map. This first reflection was almost nonexistent before the 1990s. The second way is to assist learning mirrors in how we learn think by drilling, exploring, connecting, and, now, much more. Hypercard, science tutorials, and reading drills are early examples of innovations in learning through computers. Both ways are hypermirrors: one of what is known, and the other of how the knowledge holds together and links to other knowledge.

When compact discs (CDs) came along, educational programming picked up speed. The floppy disks they were to replace could hold a few dozen pages; the CDs could hold a few dozen books. More knowledge could be stored, and more tutorials could be distributed. Schools and families could own CDs containing educational materials such as interactive encyclopedias, collections of books, educational games, and software tutorials for math and physics. Over the past decade, thousands of instructional software programs have been authored, produced, and distributed to millions of people on CDs.

Innovations in tutoring hyperwebs proliferated on CDs: typing tutors, instructive games for little children, interactive history time lines, math problems with interactive quizzes, and much more. Mirroring of knowledge lagged. Some hardcopy encyclopedias were repositioned on CDs, and the Gutenberg volunteers continued their digitization of books. But the problem here was much like my father's basement full of patient files sitting opaquely on racks—and a little worse. You could put hundreds of CDs in a rack on the wall, but comparing the detailed contents of one to that of others was nearly impossible. At least with a real book, you could pull it off the shelf, thumb through its pages, and read it! A CD had to be inserted into the computer, booted, and then explored by clicking through pages on the monitor screen.

The great change for digital education came about when the contents of computers could be related limitlessly to the contents of other computers. Even the basic level of connectivity, when computers first began to be networked, began to mirror a structural essence of thinking. A network is a macro hypermirror, and the massive ramification of networking was to make the Internet the primary arena of knowledge. The next chapter describes the migration of knowledge onto the Internet that has made cyberspace the most elegant place—outside of the mind—to store, access, and manipulate ideas.

Phrases such as *information highway* and *knowledge explosion* miss the fact of the cascade of what humans know and think about into computers hooked up to the Internet. These terms do not suggest that the highway takes you to the knowledge. Most people know there are lots more wires for information to move around on, and lots more knowledge being generated in many fields. But the two have not yet been understood as a synergy. The potential for relating digitized knowledge meaningfully has barely been noticed. In fact, the Internet was not to become like my father's basement full of file racks that you could admire as a whole, but whose related details were impossible to access. Before discussing this in more general terms, it should be helpful to look at an example of the power of a hyperweb to reflect complex relationships in new density and intuitive clarity.

The popularity of ancestry Web sites is a direct result of the nimble new knowledge navigation opportunities offered by digital media. Web sites employ hyperlinking that was pioneered in CD authoring. In a CD encyclopedia, if the article displayed on your screen was about the Civil War, Abraham Lincoln's name in the text might provide a hyperlink to another page on the CD containing his biography. In this instance, his name in the text you were reading would be blue and/or underlined, indicating that if you moved your mouse's cursor over the president's name and clicked, the Civil War would disappear and the Lincoln page would take its place on the monitor screen. Manifestations of this simple interface tool are now connecting everything that is known in meaningful relationships. At least in a rudimentary way, these Web site methods mirror how ideas exist and are explored in our minds—and because that is so, they hold great promise for utility in education. What follows is an example of using hypermirroring to make a complex subject easier to understand and accessible to many more points of view than was possible before digital technologies.

I have in my studio five books printed in the nineteenth century about five founding families of New England, a large file drawer of papers, two loose-leaf notebooks of my research notes, four drawers of pictures, and a database created with Reunion software, together comprising a trove of information about my ancestors. Most of the pictures sat in a trunk in my grandmother's basement from 1905 until the 1970s, when my parents did some cataloging. There are papers copied from family Bibles and other records that spent most of the twentieth century in my great-aunt's attic. The family books were collected by my father over several decades. His grandmother, an intellectual and probably a classmate of Emily Dickinson's at Mount Holyoke in the 1850s, pursued the same hobby as my father, and left many records of her research. Four summers ago, I worked every weekend in the extensive genealogy collection at the New York Public Library, tracing names from the various books and papers. I identified more than fifty seventeenth-century New England families among whom I had ancestors, and I created a family tree on my computer using Reunion software. The ancestors I found included nine soldiers of the American Revolution, at least two of whom answered the alarm of April 19, 1775, sounded on the famed ride of Paul Revere. I linked back my mother's father to ancestors living on the Hudson through the nineteenth century, remembered but no longer identifiable by family records. Included in my files are papers prepared for a centennial of one set of my great-grandparents' arrival in Santa Fe in 1887.

Two centuries of knowledge had converged in my studio. My problem now became divergence. Having gathered all of these materials, I could not figure out how to make what I had available to the dozens of my relatives sharing the ancestry. At one point I showed my notebooks to my brother, who was uncharacteristically daunted by the complexity of connecting all the facts. I printed a family tree for everyone, and that they loved. The tree structure was a perfect way to show the marriage and parent–child relationships down the generations. I have tried writing some "occasional papers," featuring ancestors who were soldiers of the American Revolution, and my great-grandmother's scholarship. But these efforts barely did anything to tap the potential for relationships among people—both past people and present people. A paper on the soldiers of the Revolution on my father's side is of little interest to the dozens of descendants of my mother's soldier ancestors. The Santa Fe centennial is a terrific story, but it parallels in time adventures of other relatives who stayed east, and others who settled in Kansas. Besides the family tree, the rest of the information is in stories and pictures begging to be structured in myriad ways. Again, the tree tool worked somewhat, but there is much more to the story.

I am now putting the materials I have collected into a Web site, and my troubles are over. The family tree will soon be available online, tracking the blood relationships over time. The remainder of my family Web site uses the new, nonlinear web structures that offer limitless dimensions of relationships. Ten years ago, if I had been a trained CD producer and had had the expensive computers necessary then for the job, I could have put most of the family information on a CD, had copies made, and then mailed them to every family member. The Web site is far easier and better for many reasons. The software to build it is simple, available, and cheap. There is no limit to the number of pages I can make, as there would be with a CD. As more ancestors are discovered, they can be added.

The vision that my father was pursuing with orthopaedic diagnosis and McBee Cards would have flourished in a Web site. Thinking back to our definitions based on the flow among brain synapses, *convergence* is coming together to a common point and *divergence* is the moving out from a common point in different directions. Today, facts about a particular diagnosis from diverse orthopaedic patient histories could be converged into a single Web page, where illuminating comparisons would thrive. Different Web pages for different diagnoses can be interrelated in limitless ways. Further, because orthopaedists across the Internet could access the Web pages synthesizing the diagnoses, the medical knowledge would be diverged into the active practice of doctors around the world.

We will never know whether CDs and unnetworked school computers could have played a major part in twenty-first-century education, for they have little remaining relevance. Hypermirroring has become hyperwired.

NOTES

1. *Merriam-Webster's Collegiate Dictionary,* 10th ed., 1997.
2. *Merriam-Webster's Third New International Dictionary,* unabridged, 1966.
3. Larry Cuban, *Teachers and Machines* (New York: Teachers College Press, 1986), 78.
4. In Sueann Abron and Kristina Hooper, *Learning with Interactive Multimedia* (Redmond, Wash.: Microsoft Press, 1990).
5. "Everybody Can Read: The Infinitely Patient Computer," *New York Times,* 27 September 1996.

7

Hyperwired

The Great Change became inevitable when computers began to communicate with each other. The digital soup had provided a code universally understood by computers. As computers began to exchange data, ideas could begin to converge in one machine, and ideas could diverge to other machines. Hyperwebs started connecting things in many ways, breaking out of linear ruts. Hypermirrors established rich environments where numbers, words, and images could be assembled in myriad ways. Until networking began, sharing information among computers required copying it to a disk, physically removing the disk from the originating machine, inserting the disk into the receiving machine, and then uploading the information into the receiving computer.

But then came computers that were servers: they served files to other machines through connecting wires. The sharing began in small ways that were internal to organizations and projects. I watched the hooking-up at the large Wall Street law firm where I worked during the 1970s and 1980s. The firm was one of the first to acquire a central computer for word processing, something lawyers do in enormous quantity. The word processor was actually a single computer: a mainframe that used great big reels of magnetic tape to store document texts. Wired to the mainframe from locations throughout the several floors occupied by the firm were secretarial workstations. The secretaries could input and edit documents at their desks, viewing their work interfaced from the big computer on to their monitor screens. It was one computer with many keyboards.

In the late 1980s, the firm gave individual computers to the secretaries, as well as to the lawyers, and began to store the documents in other computers, the servers. When a document was created, the work was done in the computer at the desk of the secretary or lawyer and then sent to the server. If another lawyer wanted to work on the document, she could bring it into her computer, make revisions, and send it back to the server. By the time this network had been set up at the firm, the networked search service Lexis was available in the office's library.

Lawyers could use the Lexis terminal to contact computers in Ohio, where statutes and cases were constantly being digitized and stored. It was not long after the lawyers got computers at their desks before they were hooked up to Lexis as well as to the firm's servers. They could go into a computer in Ohio, highlight and copy the text of the wording of a case, open the file of their brief downloaded from the firm's server, and there paste the wording from the case at the relevant point in their brief. An obvious change here is that the texts involved only had to be typed once—the text copied from Lexis could have been typed months or years before, and the text of the brief did not have to be retyped because of the insertion of new words. Greater even than the efficiency derived from not retyping the words were the advantages gained from connecting things in new ways.

But what was more important, the computers were hyperwired. The mainframe hub was replaced by a network in which computers were wired to each other individually. The secretaries' and lawyers' computers were wired to the server and the lawyers' machines were wired to Lexis. The server was wired to many other secretaries and lawyers, who were also wired to each other and (the lawyers) to Lexis. Lexis was wired to libraries and lawyers all over the planet. Linearity was gone, and wiring was hyper. The gift of hyperwiring was first of all access. But there was more.

Hyperwebs began functioning outside of a single computer, causing the rise of hypermirrors of high enough resolution to begin to reflect human ideas. We are being mechanical here, not mystical. The point is that ideas are formed in our minds by connecting things. When computers began to be connected by hyperwires, the things contained in different computers could be converged into one place, another computer. Those of us who did our college research in the stacks of libraries, where we hand-copied (no Xerox yet) excerpts from this book and that book, did our converging back at the dormitory. Connecting the scraps in our minds and on our notes, we typed up our ideas into a term paper. Today, a student can pull the excerpts up on his screen from different books and from different libraries. He can connect more things, and that is hyperwired access. He can also connect the ideas in limitless ways, and that hypermirrors his ideas—something that reflects ideas in the mind, at least in a rudimentary way.

The Internet is simply an enormous system of hyperwiring. Any computer can be connected to any other computer. The Internet is technically nothing but a communications hookup. It is not different in principle from the way telephones were wired over the twentieth century, and, in fact, operates now in large part over the telephone system. The telephone system is hyperwired, with any given telephone reachable from any other telephone. The telephone instrument that we talk into is limited to transmitting sound. The Internet uses the hyperwired telephone system to connect the digital information in one computer to the digital information in any other computer. As computers filled with knowledge have been connected to the Internet, individuals who have their computers connected to the Internet have access to the remote computers and to the knowledge they contain.

The stupendous new access to more knowledge by more people is by itself transforming education. If physically possible, which, of course, it is not, the access could have been achieved by some sort of warp-speed vehicle issued to everyone on Earth, so each of us could visit any library or other place where knowledge could be found whenever we wanted to. But the thousands of people who visit the Library of Congress Web site every day would not fit in the great building at the top of Capitol Hill in Washington, D.C., and if dozens of them wanted the same book at the same time, many would have to wait a very long time. The general understanding of the great value of this new access to knowledge on the Internet is growing.

What are the implications of the advent of the Internet for learning and education? What effects have been felt already? There is a great deal of confusion, because when the subject comes up, people usually start talking about a lot of different things. Some immediately begin defending teachers as better than computers for teaching. Many hold that computers should be harnessed to do school administrative tasks. To move ahead here, the distinction must be made between computers as teachers and the Internet as access to what is known. The former may be as difficult as making computers think, and may lie far in the future. The latter is already here. My opinion is that computers do not replace teachers, but instead are making classroom teaching fun again. In the final chapter I tell you why.

But first I tell you about what I have been watching unfold over the past four years, as the Internet has become the mirror for human knowledge. As I write this, I realize that what I describe is little known or understood in the year 2000. But I am not making predictions in the descriptions that follow. In fact, I have made every effort not to exaggerate. I have explored the wired world, visited the radiant medium, and observed the birth and adolescence of the Grand Idea. What follows in this chapter and the next describes what has happened in the past several years. In the final two chapters I will tell you what I think will happen inevitably as the hypermirroring radiance comes to reflect the Grand Idea. If you are to see the vision described at the close of this book, it is necessary to be aware of the extent to which knowledge can now be accessed and learned through the Internet.

Because the Internet is a communications hookup, users naturally accessed it early on to look things up. This obvious usefulness of the Internet was realized from long before its actual inception, as this excerpt from the Internet Society states:

> The first recorded description of the social interactions that could be enabled through networking was a series of memos written by J. C. R. Licklider of MIT in August 1962 discussing his "Galactic Network" concept. He envisioned a globally interconnected set of computers through which everyone could quickly access data and programs from any site. In spirit, the concept was very much like the Internet of today.[1]

Licklider foresaw the power of access, which has now reached global if not yet galactic proportions. There are many excellent descriptions of the technical steps that were made during the three decades between Licklider's early memos and the Internet's dramatic entrance as the major player in accessing knowledge. It is completely unnecessary for those of us who are not schooled in electronics and communication theory to understand the technology of the Internet. Many intelligent people have tried to figure out what the Internet is and struggled through pages of jargon laced with obfuscation, and given up. Suffice it to say that by the early 1990s the technology was in place for the Internet to become a new and powerful method for storing and accessing knowledge. It was a turning point, something like what happened when Henry Ford started rolling Model Ts off the assembly line, and the automobile really worked better than the horse and buggy for the majority of people. Just as the Model T was improved significantly in the years that followed its introduction, the Internet today is far faster and more powerful than it was a decade ago, when it first turned the corner to become the best place to put and access human ideas outside of the mind.

When the technology was sufficient to the task, a major movement to put knowledge resources into sites accessible through the Internet was born. The cumulative effect of this process has been to digitize and place online a high percentage of all printed publications, including a greater collection of books than was ever assembled at the library of Alexandria. In Internet circles this first major content migration into cyberspace is called "repositioning." Repositioning is a natural response to the invention of a new medium. When Johannes Gutenberg got his press working, the first content he printed was the Bible. Other already existing books followed. Repositioning is soon joined by innovation made possible by tools of a new medium. The printing press led to replacing the town crier with a newspaper, which could print overnight far more words than could be shouted effectively in the streets—and many more words than could be written onto paper by hand, especially overnight. The first phase of the knowledge content growth on the Internet was repositioning. Most of what was repositioned was text, which could be downloaded by remote computers in a reasonable length of time. Advancing technology has made transfer times faster, significantly increasing the size of what can be quickly accessed from the Internet.

Michael Hart had a very good idea in 1971. He was given a block of the spare time available on the Xerox Sigma V mainframe computer at the Materials Research Lab at the University of Illinois. The computer's spare time was allotted to workers to use however they chose, as a way to let them increase their proficiency with the machine. Hart foresaw that computers could be the means for the storage, retrieval, and searching of what was stored in libraries. He used his time on the mainframe to type in the Declaration of Independence. It was the beginning of what became an ongoing digitization project. Volunteers have typed vast numbers of books into computers, thus turning them into zeros and ones that could be used by any other computer to reproduce the books. At first the project's books were shared on floppy disks, and then on CDs. They became early content for the infant Internet, and the files remain in use. The Project Gutenberg Web site describes Hart's good idea in these words:

> The premise on which Michael Hart based Project Gutenberg was: anything that can be entered into a computer can be reproduced indefinitely . . . what Michael termed "Replicator Technology." The concept of Replicator Technology is simple; once a book or any other item (including pictures, sounds, and even 3-D items can be stored in a computer), then any number of copies can and will be available. Everyone in the world, or even not in this world (given satellite transmission) can have a copy of a book that has been entered into a computer.[2]

In the early 1990s, just before the Internet began to take off, a lot of knowledge resources were being repositioned onto CDs. The first of these I had was a collection of great books. It was pure text, but the text was searchable. I could enter "Longfellow" in a search box, and up would come a list of some of his famous poems. Clicking on the name of a poem would display its full text on my screen. I could drag my cursor over any of the text I wanted, press a function key on my keyboard to copy it, go to a page in my word processor, press a function key to paste it—and a fully typed version of what I had copied was placed on my page and could be saved inside my own computer. CDs seemed destined to be a major force in research and education. They looked like they would become the medium of divergence for knowledge.

There are several ways the Internet is better than CDs for accessing and using knowledge. In the matter of repositioning existing knowledge, the difficulty was that there never seemed to be enough. Once I had some of Longfellow's poems, I wanted the rest. If I wanted to compare him to his contemporaries, I would most likely be back at the bricks-and-mortar library looking for books. The need for memory in using digital technologies can be compared to the human talent for adjusting to making more money, and the inability to settle for a lower income once a higher one has been experienced. The move from floppy disks to CDs was like that. There was a time that having an entire twenty-page report on one floppy disk seemed luxurious. But a CD could hold several books, and suddenly one report was frustratingly inflexible. Yet the CDs had a limitation that the floppies did not have: the CD is a one-way street. The floppy can be added to and revised. The CD is etched by a laser when it is manufactured, and it cannot be changed. Many of the arguments and opinions about the usefulness of computers were formed in the 1980s and early 1990s. Frustrations and doubts are understandable in the environment of limited computer memory and awkward disk swapping.

After the technology was up and working by the early 1990s, and the realization dawned that it had become the best place to store and access knowledge, a huge transition began. A metaphor I like for the repositioning of knowledge onto the Internet is the cascade caused by the spring melt of snow in the mountains. With early April warmth, trickles begin, more sun brings streams that enter rivers, the rivers speed downhill and spread to their banks, the flood reaches the coastline and enters an ocean. By early summer, the moisture that piled up in the winter as snow in mountains has moved into a new, oceanic venue. The metaphor ends there, because the spring cascade from the mountains is repeated every year. That will not happen with the flood of human ideas in the form of stored knowledge. It will remain in its new cyberocean home, thriving there as in no previous medium.

The early trickles of knowledge repositioning came from sources older than the Internet proliferation. Project Gutenberg moved online, and materials that had been repositioned on CDs flowed naturally onto the Internet. Visionaries soon began thinking up new ways to use the Internet to access knowledge. One of them was Tim Berners-Lee, who now holds the 3Com Founders chair at the Laboratory for Computer Science at the Massachusetts Institute of Technology. He is the inventor of the World Wide Web. Berners-Lee also invented the Virtual Library, the oldest catalog of the Web. As the Virtual Library states:

> Unlike commercial catalogs, [the Virtual Library] is run by a loose confederation of volunteers, who compile pages of key links for particular areas in which they are expert; even though it isn't the biggest index of the web, the VL pages are widely recognized as being amongst the highest-quality guides to particular sections of the web. . . . Individual indexes live on hundreds of different servers around the world.[3]

The Virtual Library and the development of search engines were ways to find material to study as it was moving online. The wonderful synergy had begun between repositioning knowledge resources into Web sites and the means for searching and locating useful materials. Soon there were widening streams of new repositioning, as great storehouses like the Library of Congress began to open their doors to researchers who entered their newly created virtual stacks from the World Wide Web. As more people discovered the Internet as a place to find what they wanted to learn, more holders of knowledge were placing their expertise into Web sites. The rivers were flowing by the late 1990s and surging as the new millennium was born.

Early on, I mentioned the blind men who were taken one by one to feel different parts of an elephant. When they were asked as a group to describe what they had learned, one said the elephant was like a tree, because he had put his arms around a leg. Another described the beast in terms of its tail, the others in terms of its trunk and its tusk. The way the world perceives repositioned knowledge on the Internet in the year 2000 is much the same as the blind men's perception of the elephant. A delightful paradigm shift lies ahead, and what will be understood when it happens is gigantic, like an elephant, and elegant, like an idea.

When the river of knowledge began rushing to the Internet, it was fed by many, many sources. A favorite example of mine is the home pages of the various states of the United States. By the fall of 1997, each of the fifty states had a Web site. These home pages typically featured a big photograph of the governor, smiling.

There would be a logo with the state seal. Perhaps a dozen pages could be accessed from the home page. Most of those pages were all text, giving lists of state agencies and services. Two years later, the state Web sites had grown to dozens of pages. They included authoritative histories of the state. Many of them included sections designed to teach children about the state. The histories and pages for children are a completely new and up-to-date resource for education that is free to students and schools.

Over the same time that the state Web sites were developing, home pages for just about every country in the world appeared online. In 1998, I spent some time looking at the Web sites of each of the countries of the former Soviet Union. Turkmenistan had a delightful home page dominated by a photograph of a young man astride a magnificent rearing white horse. I learned that the steed was an akhalteke, the same breed as Buccephalus, the favorite horse of Alexander the Great. The few pages of the Turkmenistan site provided some basic facts about the country and its heritage. I noted at the time that the map on the home page was from a digitized collection at the University of Texas, and was displayed by hyperlink from Austin. Now, two years later, Turkmenistan's Web presence in English is an attractive and complex group of pages from its embassy in Washington. Included are sections on history and culture, government and politics, business and the economy, news, tourism and travel, and visa regulations. Two clicks into the history and culture section is the picture of the young man on his rearing horse. The essay about the akhalteke is much longer. From my later visit to the page I learned a lot more about these beautiful and historic creatures:

> The akhalteke is an ancient breed from one of the four horse types that crossed the Bering Strait from the Americas in prehistoric times. Approximately 10,000 years ago, as desertification took hold of Central Asia, the stocky horses indigenous to its Steppe grasslands began to evolve into the lean and graceful but hardy horses that inhabit Turkmenistan today. As food and water became more scarce the heavy frame of the horse gave way to a lighter one. Longer necks, a higher head carriage, larger eyes and longer ears evolved to better the ability to see, smell, and hear predators over the increasingly open plains. The golden coloring predominant among the akhalteke provided the necessary camouflage against the desert landscape. Through natural selection a breed was created which would become the pride of Turkmenistan.[4]

The preceding words were not typed by me. I copied them from the Turkmenistan Embassy Web site displayed on my monitor screen, and then pasted them into my manuscript. They were probably typed originally by someone who knew a lot about Turkmenistan and akhalteke horses. The knowledge contained in the words is an example of how knowledge resides on the Internet. It is in the digital soup, having been entered once in a computer somewhere into zeros and ones. It is part of a hypermirror as it links to other Turkmenistan topic pages. It is hyperwired through the Web address of the embassy's Web site out onto the Internet.

The Web sites of states and countries are examples of many types of sources that feed the river of knowledge being digitized and flowing onto the Internet. The new digital materials that are useful for learning academic subjects are but a small part of the deluge of other things pouring into cyberspace. As the Turkmenistan Embassy pages illustrate, the edifying page about horses was among historical materials that represented less than ten percent of the full content of the Web site. It is important to understand that home pages are receding from importance on the Internet. Hyperlinking for all sorts of pages is based on relevance, not the origin of the pages. In a noneducation example, a passport agency could link to the visa regulations section of the Turkmenistan site. An overseas business directory could link to the business and economy section. Students of Asian history and horses could link to the akhalteke page.

Finding favorite links for subjects related to a Web page is a long-standing routine on the Web. The practice has become very important to locating the knowledge you are looking for. In narrow fields of study there has been a growing tendency for the specialists around the world to get and stay linked to each other. Web rings have sprung up to establish links among all sorts of topics, including some that are studied in school. A factor of excellence in the interlinking has been the pages of college instructors, where they have included links that they have evaluated and found deserving for their fields. The Victorian Web is a large and venerable example of the convergence of resources on a topic into one Web site from which the knowledge diverges to users who follow the listed Web addresses out to resources scattered through many universities, libraries, and other repositories. A December 1999 report on the Web site of the Victorian Web shows many days with more than two thousand Internet users coming to the site to acquire knowledge about the Victorian era.[5]

Feeding each other, the repositioning of knowledge materials and the hyperwebbing of these materials crested great rivers flowing into the cyberocean. The following paragraphs give an overview of some of the major players in repositioning onto the Internet materials appropriate for academic study. Most of the players have Web sites with many other materials in addition to the academic ones. That fact does not take anything away from the information useful for learning and teaching, but rather adds to the authority, authenticity, and freshness of the material.

The U.S. government has gotten into repositioning knowledge online in a big way. The White House created and maintains a large Web site that includes officials and biographies of all the presidents and first ladies. Occupying cyberspace from Capitol Hill are thousands of pages from both legislative branches. Years ago, when I was studying American government and teaching high school civics, a standard resource for information on the U.S. Congress was the *Congressional Directory*. Here, from the Web site of the Government Printing Office, is an explanation of how the *Congressional Directory* is published now:

> Subsequent to delivery of the printed 1997–1998 Congressional Directory, the Joint Committee on Printing established the practice of producing periodic online interim

issues to ensure the public's economical access to current Congressional information. The frequency of these online revisions will be determined by the volume of changes submitted for incorporation. No printed counterpart will exist for these online publication revisions but when a new printed publication is required, the process will be greatly simplified due to the existence of the updated versions.[6]

Thus it is possible to access the entire *Congressional Directory* through the Internet. As soon as there are updates, which can be made immediately to the Web version, the online version will be more correct that the printed one. The online version can be downloaded into a portable document format (PDF) so that your computer can print them. By doing that, you would have a fresher printed version of the directory than the one produced by the print publisher. As this process begins to be applied to school textbooks, students will have study materials that are the freshest and most accurate in the history of education.

The congressional Web sites have extensive explanations of how laws are made, along with ways to follow the passage of legislation. The U.S. Supreme Court Web site describes the Court and explains how it does its work, and provides access to its docket, rules, opinions, history, and more. Maturing Web sites for each cabinet-level agency, armed service, and other government entities pour knowledge about themselves and the areas of their responsibility into the Internet. The mammoth National Aeronautics and Space Administration (NASA) Web pages contain dozens of scientific subjects, illustrated with images from space and replete with records of the development of satellites and shuttles. The Web site of the U.S. Geological Survey is a large labyrinth of environmental and geographical topics that richly reposition a great deal of material on subjects that run the gamut from elementary general science to graduate-level specialties. The National Gallery displays its American art treasures online. The Smithsonian Institution is working to digitize all of its collections.

Colleges and universities are putting pages and projects online that showcase their academic specialties and institutional treasures. These Web pages take a number of different forms. Some are the lecture notes of professors and instructors, placed on the Internet with syllabi for their students. Others are departmental projects that illustrate and explain research. Some universities have created collections of materials and links that have made them the place to go on the Internet for a particular area of research. Others have digitized and placed online collections of maps and artifacts.

Libraries and museums have dabbled with the Internet since it began to grow prominent. Many library catalogs are available online, providing bibliographies for subjects if not the texts of the works themselves. Increasingly, libraries are offering online exhibits and access to texts. Beginning in 1999, museums everywhere have gotten the Internet bug in a big way. Their collections are flowing into some of the most beautiful sites on the entire Web. Speedier connections and better tools for digital image making have made this new access to the visual arts possible. Libraries are using these new methods as well, exhibiting images of original documents, where often you can zoom in to read words written by hand decades or centuries ago.

Active science is another major new area of access to knowledge made possible by the Internet. Knowledge can now be studied and learned as it is created. The Web pages describing the exploration of the human genome are renewed on a daily basis. Web sites are made for probes into space months or years before liftoff, and they continue during and after the mission. Archaeological digs can be followed for weeks and months. Zoo animals can be observed through live cameras, and animal projects in the wild can be tracked as they occur. Weather events can be observed from all sorts of perspectives, with explanations by scientists accompanying the views.

We are used to following developments in the newspapers or on television. There is a huge advantage for learning to tracking active science on an Internet site. As things happen, the older media report them, and the report then goes into the paper recycling or into the tape archives at the television studio. On an Internet site, not only can you access the reporting at any time, day or night, the knowledge reports build a study resource. On a space shuttle Web site, the pages remain accessible from all of the stages and events. The Web site is a real-time study source as things develop, and it then transforms into a permanent history of the event.

Expert organizations constitute yet another important and authoritative group that is repositioning knowledge onto the Internet. Some of the government agencies fall into this category, but there are many more. When an expert entity builds a Web site about itself, it wants to give its background and present its area of expertise. Web sites of this sort are usually well-funded and well-done. The results are excellent pages of history or explanations of operations that are accurate, authoritative, interesting, and free to students and teachers. Many corporate and trade Web sites have backgound pages with descriptions of their histories. Not long ago I looked through the Web sites of the major labor unions in the United States. Many of them had histories of their unions, with pages that included historical photographs and narratives. Another time I looked through all of the associations of livestock breeders and found many pages on the history of different breeds of horses, cattle, sheep, goats, and chickens. Although some might be suspect of the objectivity of businesses, trade associations, and unions, I can assure you that the livestock descriptions were grade-A educational materials. Many included "kids" pages with elementary materials. The suspicion that entity Web sites are unreasonably skewed to a point of view is valid. However, the fact that students using them have gone to a source with an obvious point of view is a key tool for teaching critical thinking.

Most attempts to describe what is happening on the Internet quickly turn into laundry lists. I will not go on except to say that there are many more sources for interesting and useful knowledge now repositioned on the Internet. As the new millennium arrived, the great meltdown of my metaphor had caused a wide flow to further levels of new detail, across deltas from which the repositioned knowledge is entering the cyberocean. Once, it seemed significant that all the U.S. states had home pages, and now all the national parks and most of the state parks do. State historical markers are getting their own pages. City and town historical societies are digitizing documents and photographs only seen by a few local history buffs over the years, and making them available to the world. Endless scientific databases and image banks have come online, and are kept up-to-date only digitally. In almost every academic field the trend is the same.

The Internet is, or very soon will be, the primary location of human knowledge. Does that mean the end of books and libraries? It is hard to say, but do focus on the word "primary." There are many advantages to letting the Internet be the primary location for knowledge. The important handbook for legislators, the *Congressional Directory*, shows us one of the advantages. Any time you want a printed version of that book you can have it by going to the Internet, downloading it, and printing either all of it or just what you happen to need at the time.

As the primary location of knowledge has become the Internet, instead of less flexible media, we have been surprised by unplanned advantages for learning and teaching. Remote updating is one of those wonderful things you do not know how you got along without once you start using it. It makes textbooks in classrooms in 2000 that still have the Soviet Union as a world power intolerable. There are several Web sites that list the official governments of countries around the world. Whenever there is an election or coup d'état, the Webmasters make appropriate changes in the listings. How did we check those things before the Internet came along?

Another interesting aspect of accessing knowledge through the Internet is the ease with which original resources can be studied. This not only applies to images of documents digitized from libraries. The excerpt below is from the official Web site of the government of Tibet in exile. It says in the biography of the Dalai Lama:

> His Holiness follows the life of Buddhist monk. Living in a small cottage in Dharamsala, he rises at 4 A.M. to meditate, pursues an ongoing schedule of administrative meetings, private audiences and religious teachings and ceremonies. He concludes each day with further prayer before retiring. In explaining his greatest sources of inspiration, he often cites a favorite verse, found in the writings of the renowned eighth century Buddhist saint Shantideva:
>
> > For as long as space endures
> > And for as long as living beings remain,
> > Until then may I too abide
> > To dispel the misery of the world.[7]

You could read somewhere or hear from someone that the Dalai Lama has this routine and says these words. Accessing this page from the Internet is somewhat like watching a television interview of the Tibetan monk, but the page has an ongoing live presence in the Web site. Any time he wants to, the Dalai Lama can change the page. There is a new intimacy here. I was struck by this when the king of Jordan died. The official Web site had featured many wonderful pictures and stories of the much-loved king. It was many days after his death before the Web site was changed at all. It must have been difficult and painful to make the eventual changes. There is richness here for students. They can travel virtually to all sorts of new repositories of ideas. Darius never even heard of his contemporaries Confucius and Buddha. The last year all three were still alive, Pericles was the age of today's middle school students. With the Internet he could have accessed the thoughts of three people whose ideas still shape our world. I suspect middle schoolers today are already doing that sort of thing.

It will not be long before almost everything that was ever known will be available on the Internet. It will be summer, and all of the flow from the mountains of accumulated human knowledge will be finished. What will be missing from the Internet will be missing because nobody knows it anymore. Atlantis remains pretty well lost, but everything that is known and speculated about it will soon be available to everyone on Earth through the Internet. Not only that, but new discoveries are now beginning to be found only on the Internet. A good example is active archaeological Web sites that are kept up-to-date with new discoveries. Those discoveries will be online months or years before they are published in print, and they may never be printed. The same phenomenon in fast-moving sciences, such as genetics, has made the Web the primary resource for the current state of the science. No book ever written will capture the accounts of the road construction projects called the "Big Dig" in Boston and the "Big I" in Albuquerque. The Web sites of these enormous endeavors explain the engineering, record the progress, and let you watch what is being done through live cameras. We can only muse about what the Great Pyramid must have looked like while it was being built. Construction behemoths of the present and future can be observed in real time and kept online for future study.

The primary location of knowledge is the Internet, and more and more knowledge can be found only there. These are huge changes with enormous impact. But they are only part of a bigger story. Less noticed than the access is the connecting—the hyperwebbing—out on the Internet that is transforming knowledge and will profoundly affect education in the future. Convergence is a fundamental principle of brain organization and is the ghost that haunts us from the library of Alexandria. As we enjoy the connecting of things to create an idea in our minds, relationships spontaneously arise and lead us to wander mentally down related paths to other concepts and memories. To the degree that convergence is integral to hyperwebs, divergence is equally present. On the Internet, pieces of human knowledge are coming together and spreading out at warp speed. Everything known by humankind is migrating into the Internet, where paths of relationships are linking troves of ideas. This is not science fiction. It is the new reality.

The approaching access by everybody to everything that is known is a profoundly important turn of events for humankind. Less realized, and a change that is at least as fundamental, is that ideas within the knowledge accessed from the Internet are being reflected in new ways that begin to approximate how we think about them. The next chapter explores how imaginative people are exploiting the nonlinear opportunities in the digital soup to allow us to interface with knowledge in ways that help us better understand and learn.

NOTES

1. "A Brief History of the Internet," *Internet Society* <http://www.isoc.org/internet-history/brief.html#Introduction>, 4 August 2000 [accessed 3 August 2000].

2. "History and Philosophy of Project Gutenberg," *Project Gutenberg* <http://promo.net/pg/history.html#beginning>, August 1992 [accessed 3 August 2000].

3. "About the Virtual Library," *The WWW Virtual Library* <http://vlib.org/AboutVL.html> 12 March 2000 [accessed 3 August 2000].

4. "The Akhalteke Horse of Turkmenistan," *Embassy of Turkmenistan* <http://www.turkmenistanembassy.org/turkmen/history/horses.html>, 18 September 2000 [accessed 23 October 2000].

5. *Victorian Web Research,* <http://www.indiana.edu/~victoria/nisdata/stats-page.html>, 11 January 2000 [accessed 3 August 2000].

6. *Congressional Directory,* <http://www.access.gpo.gov/congress/cong016.html>, 29 March 2000 [accessed 3 August 2000].

7. "The Dalai Lama's Biography," *The Government of Tibet in Exile* <http://www.tibet.com/DL/biography.html>, 9 September 1997 [accessed 3 August 2000].

8

New Reflections

The placement of typed books onto Web sites simply repositioned them from the print medium to the digital medium. The ideas contained in the books were still read as text from the monitor screen. Connections among the ideas were made in the reader's mind, just as if she were reading a printed book. But something different happened when words on the screen's text became hyperlinked. If the online book used difficult words, they could be underlined in the text, clicked, and the glossary definition of the word would pop up. This was a lot handier than locating a dictionary and looking up the word. Other underlined words or phrases could transport the reader to relevant pages within the same online book. All of these things, of course, could be done on CDs. When the Internet came along, however, it became possible to hyperlink text to any other page on the Internet. If the text was about akhalteke horses in Turkmenistan, the name of the country could be hyperlinked, and the reader could access the Turkmenistan page about the horses. The signal from Turkmenistan bounced around the planet, through wires and off of satellites, to display a page on the reader's monitor screen. This, of course, is access, but there are also powerful cognitive implications. If the reader is thinking about horses and Turkmenistan together, adjacent information about them can be mirrored from the Internet, reflecting something of the structure of her thoughts.

The connection of individuals to repositories of knowledge and then the creation of interconnections within the repositioned knowledge were the first and important phases of the development of the Internet. But more was happening. Not only were stored ideas and knowledge able to converge through the Internet. There was a parallel convergence of different kinds of media. Slowly at first, and then massively, enormous creativity was detonated by the convergence of multimedia first into computers and onto CDs, and then out to the Web. Multimedia was made possible by the digital soup: the conversion of text, images, and sounds into zeros and ones, so that the words, pictures, and noises could be combined into the same code. All of it could then be burned by a laser beam onto the surface of a CD, where the zeros and ones are represented by tiny flat spots and pits. The designers of the CDs of the 1980s pioneered multimedia authoring. By the time designers were at work, there was enough memory to create fairly complicated and attractive stuff. They, in turn, used a palette of digital tools that had evolved to replace designers' pens, brushes, metal fonts, T squares, and pigments, just as adding machines, slide rules, mechanical cash registers, and accounting ledgers had been made obsolete by digital replacements. Computer-assisted design (CAD) software became the mainstay for architectural and engineering design. Programmers used zeros and ones to animate images, replacing the thousands of original drawings for cartoon movies and making all sorts of things move on computer screens.

There are many fascinating, and to some disturbing, results and implications of the convergence of multimedia into digital form. One worry is about the impact on craft. When Rembrandt was preparing to paint, he might have to spend all morning getting his pigments ready, concocting them from azurite, chalk, cologne earth, ocher, smalt, tin, vermilion, and zinc. How much could he have painted, and what would he have produced, had the great genius been able to select from millions of colors in a few seconds, as is possible on computer software? Software paint programs offer ranges of virtual brushes, a wider choice of visual effects, and almost immediate revisions and corrections beyond what Rembrandt could have imagined in his wildest fantasies, which must have visited him during his long, tedious hours of grinding and mixing his ochers and smalts. What will the future of the visual arts lose because apprentice artists no longer have to learn the craft of mixing pigments? Will their time be better used in developing design thoughts because there is no need to clean the sticky oil out of brushes after a painting session? Will the powerful new painting tools cause more Rembrandts to come along, or will we endure a visual world online and offline where the powerful digital painting tools are used to splash amateurish and even ugly stuff all over the place? The jury still seems to be out on that one. However, the powerful new display tools developed for the visual arts and for publishing are now being put to work in a medium where they are enormously useful and effective: Web design. There is no way to apply oil paint here; everything is zeros and ones.

A Web site, just like a Rembrandt or any other painting, is created to express ideas. The aphorism from the arts, that good design does not show, applies here. What you want to get from the painting or the Web site are the ideas. The tools of display work with hyperconnecting methods to create a whole that becomes a user environment. A decade ago, hyperlinking in CDs began allowing the user to click on icons and underlined words to move around in nonlinear ways. Even before the CDs, video game producers exploited this digital action, allowing the hand on the joystick to move things around on the screen. Each CD and video game was a little universe of its own. The palette available to Web authors includes anything and everything in cyberspace, which is the entire, fast-growing Internet.

I do not have to concern myself with limits of memory or access as I build my family Web site. I can scan dozens of photographs and put them on many separate pages, linked to each other in meaningful ways. My Web pages can diverge endlessly and converge in interesting nodes, conforming to an essential characteristic of human thinking and knowledge, as well as to the fruits of my prolific New England ancestors. I can tame the files and piles of the many branches of my family by actually exploiting what Stephan Jay Gould described as knowledge's inexorable tendency to ramify as it grows.

My family Web site is a hypermirror where paths of relationships link to troves of memories and moments. My second cousin George can click twice to learn about our mutual great-grandparents' three great-grandfathers who fought the British as American Patriots. With two other clicks, my grandniece Camille can meet the nine American soldiers in her father's heritage, which include both George's Patriot ancestors and six more through my father's side. It is almost impossible to detail these relationships in text, yet they are obvious and intuitive in digital navigation. As my Web site grows, George and Camille can navigate through the knowledge of our family in many different ways. Although this kind of experience is not new to thinking or to conversation, in digital environments, such as individual computers and CDs, the experience moves dramatically beyond anything possible in print, illustration, film, or any other predigital medium. As the hypermirroring of ideas rises out of the Internet, all previous media for reflecting ideas are magnified and surpassed. My family Web site connects far beyond the hard drive of my computer. It links to a mammoth genealogical Web presence through which it connects to thousands of records. My pages about family members who fought in the Revolution are decorated with images of Mel Gibson in Patriot costume that I downloaded from the Web site advertising his movie. As my pages expand, they will connect to pages on the sites of other family members, which are, in turn, connected elsewhere on the World Wide Web.

In the same manner that the horizons of digital technical innovation and artistic design beckoned geniuses of originality in the late twentieth century, conceiving ways for people like George and Camille to be informed by a Web site has grabbed imaginations of today's Web authors. The challenges are technical, artistic, pedagogical, and above all, cognitive—following how people think. Since 1996 I have looked at thousands of Web sites to evaluate them as sources of knowledge useful to students. I have been continuously surprised and impressed by the outpouring of new ideas for interfacing knowledge from Web pages coming from software companies, commercial and institutional Web sites, and individuals.

Many times when I open a Web page to find an excellent new interface idea or design, I wish I could meet the Webmaster of that site. The originality that bubbles its way into the Internet is one of the medium's happiest aspects. When compared to television, for example, the ease of self-expression is completely at the opposite end of the spectrum of difficulty. Getting even a ten-second commercial broadcast on TV costs a great deal of money and requires writers, artists, video people, studio time, and more. The spot may run just a few times or hundreds of times, but it always comes and goes quickly, on and then off the air. Contrast television production with the ease of making a Web site. The cost for the Web site is negligible. One person can do all the creative work on a single computer, and once the Web pages go online, they can be viewed at any time by anyone anywhere. Comparing a TV spot with a Web page in another way brings good news. The cost and air time constraints of television have caused the medium to drift steadily downward in its appeal toward the lowest common denominator, because what is broadcast must appeal to the largest number of people. The opposite is true of Web sites, because they are cheap and the medium is capable of hosting virtually unlimited pages, from the collection of the Louvre to a drawing by a single kindergartner. The key to the usefulness of all of this is how things are connected to each other. But this is getting ahead of our story.

Designing Web sites has become a major new industry and hobby. The catalog of a five-day fall 2000 conference devoted to the Web divides the dozens of seminars into three tracks, and this division is instructive. The Strategy Track essentially covers the business aspects of the Internet. The Technology Track is devoted to what happens within the machines. The User Experience Track boils down to how a person sitting at a computer looking at a Web site can display and connect things meaningfully. This book is about one aspect of usability: the construction of ideas that are accessed through Web pages. The goal of the design is to mirror ideas in ways that the user can apprehend them. When the Internet was young and materials like books and pictures were simply repositioned onto Web pages that you could scroll through as you would turn the pages in a book, a very natural reaction was, "Why not just read the book?" The User Experience attendees are learning and developing completely new ways to interface ideas. When they are successful, there are ideas out there that you cannot experience except on the Web pages they build. The once-small trickle in that direction is now a gusher.

The current word *navigation* is a major consideration in designing the Web user experience. Web authors believe that users experience their Web sites as space through which they move, stopping along the way to read something, look at a picture, check a bank account, or buy something. Web pages and things on Web pages are linked in ways that allow users to move from one thing to another. These links build relationships among locations on the pages and among pages. In the first chapter, I discuss how a child forms an idea of a tree by connecting tall things, things that make shade, leaves, and the color green. Is it not possible that when users navigate through well-authored Web pages, they are connecting things mentally? Access to ideas is wonderful, and that alone is a major asset for future education. Paralleling the growth of this access is the equally marvelous development of digital interface designs that reflect ideas in ways similar to how we think them.

In tandem with burgeoning access to knowledge is the invention of new ways for mirroring of human knowledge. What follows are some observations that have occurred to me as I have watched the migration of knowledge into cyberspace for the past four years. My guess is that while the repositioning will be pretty well completed in the next few months or years, the transformation of human ideas into their new forms of reflection from the cyberspace is just beginning. Out there they can be painted with the new digital palette, linked meaningfully to each other, and ramified endlessly.

In addition to knowledge that has been repositioned from print, photography, and other older media, there is already a significant amount of knowledge that, like the movie star mouse Stuart Little, exists only digitally. In this movie, Snowbell is a flesh-and-blood cat who was captured on film, while Stuart is composed of zeros and ones. Nobody in the *Toy Story* movies is flesh and blood, not even the humans. The humans, just like Buzz Lightyear, are zeros and ones. The same is true for the Metropolitan Museum of Art's tutorial on the famous painting of *George Washington Crossing the Delaware* that hangs in hard copy in the museum's American Wing.[1] The online tutorial offers hyperwebbed pages on how the artist, Emanuel Gottlieb Leutze, used perspective, light, color, form, motion, and proportion to express a dramatic event that occurred during the American Revolution. The page about the use of motion describes how the artist deployed pictorial techniques to apply motion to the water, the boat and the soldier aboard it, and the flag. It concludes with this explanation of George Washington's pose: "General Washington appears to be the only element in the painting that does NOT move. Washington stands erect and resolute, focusing his thoughts on the future, not on the worries of the moment. His confidence is inspiring to his soldiers as they struggle against great odds to cross the icy river at dawn."[2]

This tutorial demonstrates several significant aspects of new reflection of human knowledge from the Internet. The Metropolitan Museum is repositioning treasures from its collection onto the Internet. The digital design palette has been used to create images and text online. Hyperlinking has been employed in the tutorial to allow a user to move back and forth between elements of the painting, to study them individually and to understand their relationship. The tutorial was authored in the Web medium and, like Stuart Little, exists only digitally.

One of the reasons the Internet is becoming the primary source for knowledge is because it is getting handier to put it there first. The progression is logical. Decades ago the early word processors made it necessary to type something only once. The typed work could be stored on magnetic cards at first and later on floppy disks. Mainframe computers, like the one at the law office where I worked in the 1970s, could store documents in a central computer that was connected to more than one word processing machine, and the typing was done directly into the mainframe's memory. A new convenience came about when external servers connected to typists and other computers allowed the typed documents to be downloaded into remote stations that had both a computer and a keyboard. At this point, documents could be swapped around in a closed system.

The Internet has taken another step by providing a place to create and store documents that everyone in the world can access, making the Internet not only an excellent place to store documents but to publish them in the first place. The archaeological Web sites for active digs do exactly that. As artifacts and structures are found and analyzed, what is known about them goes onto the Web site in the form of reports and pictures. The highway construction projects mentioned previously can most efficiently inform the public through the Internet because changes are happening rapidly, and time is saved by not using print media that must be distributed in hard copy. Furthermore, the reports remain available online, unlike what is reported over radio and television. If you missed the five o'clock television news, you might not know that tomorrow morning your usual ramp to the interstate will be closed. You can find that out anytime from the highway project's Web site.

As we move ahead, it is increasingly difficult, and unnecessary, to separate the two new ways the Internet has changed our interaction with knowledge. These two are, first, the fact that knowledge is now primarily located on the Internet and accessible there, and second, that the Web mirrors knowledge with exciting new reflections. Why are these two not the talk of the education world and front-page news? The answer is simple: they are not yet known. To make them known is the purpose of this book. And we can take encouragement from the word *yet*. Let me put it in perspective in terms of my metaphor about the melting of the mountain snows and their runoff into streams, rivers, and the cyberocean. While this process is far along for the migration of knowledge to the Internet, awareness is back in early April, where the snows of insight are just beginning to feel the warmth of the spring sun.

There are many reasons that the extent and quality of knowledge in cyberspace have not been generally observed. The learning curve for working with the Internet remains high. Most of those who use the Internet in more than a casual way do it for purposes not related to education. Those who research knowledge in cyberspace tend to be very specialized in small areas of study, such as archaeology of the Hittites or the phyla of ferns. This last group is using the Internet in a micro way similar to how it will soon be used in a macro way. Those who now do macro research have difficulty because of the immensity of the ocean and the diversity of its contents. Yet it is the expanding scale of diversity and complexity of the Internet that welcomes human thought, which needs a sufficiently diverse and complex matrix to be fully reflected. Within the Web, the weaving of reflected ideas must move further along before the shift from its smaller parts separately is made to understanding the whole of the Grand Idea. That will happen soon.

As progress continues toward a grander understanding of the scope of ideas reflected from the Internet, new advantages that the Internet offers for education will become apparent. I have already mentioned the freshness of the knowledge because it is updated remotely. Some other thoughts about the character and usefulness of online study resources follow.

Because Web authors build their pages as spaces to be traveled within, students find themselves able to make connections. The ubiquitous opportunities to click hyperlinked objects and pages stimulate thinking and force choices. Ideas are enriched and become interconnected by the relationships experienced in the clicking around in a well-conceived Web site. Critical thinking can produce immediate results, with a click.

There are projects on the Internet where individuals can participate over time, following the migration of birds, dragonflies, and elephants. In the Web pages that host these projects, the participants can do a variety of things, including locate and learn the history of the project, access scientific data and images of the animals, file reports of observations, and communicate by e-mail with the scientists. As the migrations progress, reports of events appear on the Web pages. The whole of the learning experience is greater than the sum of the parts. A rich hyperwebbing exists in the Web pages, reflecting into the mind an overall idea of the migration, an idea that will be enriched as the migration progresses.

In a less dramatic way, most Web sites that contain knowledge reflect significant relationships. Few sites consist only of text anymore, where you can only scroll down a page. Most include images, and these images are often clickable, giving access to a bigger picture that includes explanations and that may lead to related pages. It is routine for Web sites that focus on a particular subject to include links to other Web sites with related knowledge.

We are creatures of habit, ingrained with the idea that things will be done in the future as they were in the past. It is therefore quite natural to suppose that knowledge in cyberspace will look something like a textbook. That is not what is happening. Textbooks, or any book for that matter, are written to set out very specific hunks of knowledge, and nothing more. They may have a section of further reading, but textbooks present a prescribed set of facts, and do so with a learner in mind who is at a prescribed level of readiness to understand the materials. Although virtual textbooks that will follow this pattern are in the pipe and may have a major future online presence, the cascade of knowledge onto the Internet tends not to be focused on who should learn what, but on the knowledge itself. Certainly there are superb Web projects aimed at kids, but they represent a tiny portion of what can be used from the Internet in learning and teaching.

Knowledge itself is compelling. One look at an image from the Hubble Space Telescope or watching the inside of a beehive in real time or turning around the reconstructed three-dimensional image of the Hippodrome at Constantinople proves it. Most Web sites that contain knowledge are stimulating one-room virtual schools. A favorite example of mine for explaining this point is a map of recent earthquakes in California that displays the quakes as little squares.[3] The relative size of the squares indicates their magnitude. The yellow squares indicate earthquakes that have occurred within the past week, the blue in the last day, and the red in the last hour. The only earthquake I have ever experienced occurred when I was five years old, and I still remember it. A young student can be taught a great deal about earthquakes by a teacher who shows him how the map works and clicks some of the simpler maps with him. From grade school general science through high school earth sciences and on to college geology, this one Web site is full of ideas to learn about earthquakes and facts to include in school reports. The page contains and links to rich sources of data that graduate students can use.

The one-room school is the usual character of Web sites about ideas. Most descriptions of knowledge on the Web are focused on the subject, and on explaining it in most cases to a general audience. There is a sense in which the display of knowledge by Web sites is much like what a museum does. A museum does not alter its collections to suit its audience. It does not have a simple version of a Rembrandt painted so that the average person can understand it. The Smithsonian does not hang a scaled-down version of the Wright Brothers' *Kittyhawk*. Historic documents are not displayed in modern English. The same is true with the Web sites of many scientific laboratories that have created online pages to explain what they do. Some Web presences are hybrids in this aspect. The Colonial Williamsburg pages feature many historical facts and illustrations, but they are explained in text understandable to students who are fairly new to history.

The one-room school environment created by many Web sites on many subjects can be very useful to classroom teachers. If there is something for every level, you do not have to teach to the middle of the class. The precocious kids, who lose learning time to boredom, can push ahead to challenging materials. At the same time, those in the class who never seem to keep up can review for as long as necessary with the ever-patient computer.

From the earliest days of the development of computer interactivity and graphics, people interested in using the computer as a tutor have been coming up with good ideas. Many of these tutorials are available online. The Internet has increased the ranks of tutorial makers. The tutorials range from interactive multiplication flash cards to opuses such as the comprehensive and handsome cell biology tutorials from the University of Arizona.[4]

Internet access and digital technologies have combined to make studying some subjects anywhere but on the Internet seem archaic. A major example of this is geography. Maps that have spent decades or centuries in file drawers are now digitized and viewable on the Internet. Many can be studied more closely in digital form than on the real map because details and colors have been enhanced. Real-time geography is all over the Web, as weather reports, satellite cameras, and animations abound. Why would anyone ever want to draw a map on paper again? In the old days (a couple of decades ago), maps were printed with multiple press runs of different colors, where the details had to be perfectly registered on top of one another by the presses. Now digital maps let you select the features you want—roads, towns, rivers—from multiple available layers; check your choices, click "go," and look at the result. If you forgot you wanted lakes, check the box for lakes, click again, and the map reappears with every checked feature. In most maps of this sort, you can also click on an area of the map to zoom in for more details.

The last aspect of online knowledge to ponder before we move to what I believe lies ahead has to do, once again, with converging things. It is a phenomenon that makes research on the Internet a new and more comprehensive academic experience. As we have seen, there has been a steady and quickening flow of books into digital form and onto the Internet. Museums and libraries have added to the virtual resources. Many professors and other teachers have placed syllabi and teaching materials online. Individuals with interests in specific subjects have created Web pages about their areas of expertise, and they have listed links to other Web pages with related materials. All of these processes have become increasingly interconnected. At a micro level, academic collegiality on the Internet is firmly in place, hypermirroring academic fields of study. I am struck by the comparison between the growing connections in a toddler's mind and the growth of ideas in cyberknowledge. More about that in the last chapter.

All but the last element of the Great Change are in place. The digital soup has become a digital ocean. Hyperwebs arising from the zeros and ones have been framed into hypermirrors for ideas. The Internet has opened up vast knowledge access as a communication system and stimulated worldwide hypermirrors of ideas. I have written this book out of my amazement at how little noticed the Great Change is. Most people do not know it is happening. Many understand the technical changes, the connectedness of e-mail, and the transformation of business now under way through e-commerce. Yet what is happening to human ideas is more important and is the best news of all. The earlier portions of this book were written to lead up to what follows. I hope the discussion of how these things have gotten this far will be helpful in realizing that we are just coming over the horizon where the medium will reflect the Grand Idea. What medium? The newest surprise is that we will not have to wire the schools because we will not have to plug in the kids.

NOTES

1. "Explore and Learn: George Washington Crossing the Delaware," *The Metropolitian Museum of Art* <http://www.metmuseum.org/explore/gw/el_gw.htm> [accessed 3 August 2000].

2. "Explore and Learn," *The Metropolitian Museum of Art.*

3. "Earthquakes in California," *U.S. Geological Survey* <http://quake.wr.usgs.gov/recenteqs/> [accessed 3 August 2000].

4. "Cell Biology Problem Sets and Tutorials," *The Biology Project, University of Arizona* <http://www.biology.arizona.edu/cell_bio/cell_bio.html>, 25 March 1999 [accessed 3 August 2000].

9

The Radiant Medium

The *Intrepid*'s stalwart profile juts out toward midtown Manhattan from a berth on the Hudson River, just below the ocean liner pier to the north where the QE2 docks. The grand old warship saw action and took fire in World War II, the Korean War, and the war in Vietnam. Now too out-of-date for sea duty, the *Intrepid* is an enormous space and air museum that towers over sister exhibit ships and displays a deck full of twentieth-century military aircraft. The 107.4-foot-long, 18.5-foot-high silhouette of an SR-71 Blackbird perches on the profile of the bow deck.

Because technology found a far better way to do what the airplane was designed for, the SR-71 is out of service and obsolete. It achieved heights and speeds so far not exceeded by any other production aircraft. It can fly at three times the speed of sound, and it set the world absolute and class speed record at 2,194 miles per hour in 1976. That same year it set the high-altitude record by sustaining horizontal flight at 85,069 feet. The SR-71 was built and used for broad-area stealth reconnaissance. It was equipped with an optical bar camera and a technical objective camera wet film system. The Blackbirds flew high and far during the Cold War to capture images for U.S. military and intelligence agencies. The aircraft became obsolete when satellites could go higher and see farther. The satellites replaced the SR-71's wet photography with zeros and ones captured by orbiting cameras and transmitted back to installations on Earth, where the digital code was converted by computers into images.

Our access to the Internet is about to make a similar big shift to something better. I first learned of it from Apple Chief Executive Officer Steve Jobs. He was speaking to several thousand Macintosh computer enthusiasts in the cavernous Javits Center, which sits next to the Hudson River twelve blocks south of the *Intrepid*'s berth. The long line for the event got me in late, and I watched from a seat near the back. Most of what I saw was on the large monitors placed around the hall, where what was happening onstage was projected. Looking between two pillars I could see Jobs in the distance. His presentation was very long and very well-received. He built the excitement, announcing and explaining one new product after another. The climax was the unveiling of the laptop version of the very popular and colorful iMacs. Jobs pulled the new machine out from behind the lectern, and then told us its name: iBook. For many minutes he described the new laptop Mac, often going beyond my technical understanding, but very much pleasing the many tech people in the audience. My attention had drifted when I heard a few, and then more, people around the hall beginning to clap, and then whistle, and then cheer. Their man Steve was passing an iBook back and forth from one hand to the other through a hula hoop. I think he had to say it before I caught on: there were no wires. His iBook was receiving the Internet wirelessly from a transmitter twenty feet away. This was SR-71 versus satellite stuff. Everything had changed: we can access ideas reflected from everywhere without plugging into a wire.

The early history of access to the reflection of ideas outside of the human mind is a series of new media inventions: language, pictorial symbols, written language, printed pictorial and language symbols. Distance has always caused problems. The Tree of the Knowledge of Good and Evil was left behind in the gardens of our origins. How odd that of all living creatures, we developed the capacity for symbolic language, and yet spread ourselves throughout our planet, forgetting how to talk to each other as our brothers and sisters wandered over the mountains and beyond the seas. Things did not get much better when written languages came along. Most of the early written languages were lost to our understanding for millennia, or forever. The progress of writing down ideas was not neat and pretty. We can be too quick to think about languages and writing by hanging their stories on the handy model of the tree structure. A book prepared in 1999 by the British Museum for the two hundredth anniversary of the discovery of the Rosetta Stone includes this caution:

> The prominence of the alphabet in the modern world favors the assumption that it is inherently the best writing system, but this is not the case, even though many studies such as *The Triumph of the Alphabet* have presented the history of writing as an evolution towards the modern, primarily Western, ideal. This evolutionary model can suggest that the birth of writing was a single event, and it has sometimes been maintained that all forms of early script in the ancient Near East were derived from a single 'discovery' or 'invention'.[1]

There are many fascinating theories and ongoing studies of language origins. The author of the above passage is Richard Parkinson, assistant keeper of the Department of Egyptian Antiquities at the British Museum. He doubts that all writing systems branched out from one, and concludes: "The predominance, or 'triumph,' of the alphabet is due to the cultural fortunes of the users of the alphabet rather than to the inherent superiority of the system."[2] None of the confusion of its history should take away from the realization that the single good idea of writing things down was key to the preservation of human knowledge over time. Stories had persisted, passed down from parent to child, for dozens of generations; when writing was invented, the stories were chiseled and inscribed—and hard copy was born. Great ideas had been thought of at one side of a continent but remained in the isolation of distance from people on the other side of the land and sea. Writing meant ideas could travel independently of what people could remember, on the backs of people and camels and over the water in boats. Yet, what was written down entered avenues of chaotic preservation and most often deteriorated in melting clay tablets or went up in the smoke of burning papyrus scrolls.

Printing magnified the power of writing. In a great technical innovation, writing with quill in hand was replicated by a machine. Books were printed and books were burned, and then printed and not burned. Once books took hold, they became the repository of knowledge, scattered in libraries and possessed by more and more people over the last five centuries.

Human knowledge survived, at least in part, before printing. As printing developed, knowledge began, in bits and starts, to grow and diverge. Very few of the people who lived before 1900 knew how to read. During the twentieth century, technologies were created that enhanced both the convergence of knowledge and its placement into safer storage, and accelerated its divergence to more people in more places. These new media impacted things in various ways. World War II was in part generated by Adolf Hitler's voice blasting through amplifiers to thousands gathered in Nuremberg's Reichsparteitagsgelände and simultaneously to millions of others over the radio. Tokyo Rose's radio broadcasts undermined the morale of Allied troops in the Pacific. The voices of Winston Churchill and Franklin Roosevelt carried by radio to the British and Americans were factors in winning the war. Television and satellite transmission set in motion cascading changes in the decades after the war. By the end of the twentieth century, there was a knowledge explosion ignited by the globalization of analog media and the advent of digital media.

The Great Change we are now about to see completed began by the digitizing of knowledge into zeros and ones, out of which rose hyperwebbed mirrors of all sorts of knowledge, and then this universally exchangeable knowledge migrated onto the hyperwired Internet. Now, in the final step, the need for wiring at the user end is disappearing as the Internet begins radiating from local antennas. Once again, there is a surprise in the history of human ideas, and this one is the best of all. The whole world now has a universal code that can represent every existent symbol, and therefore can represent anything people have ever written, sounded, or imaged. Computers store and interface these symbols. The Internet provides addresses for millions and millions of computers. New wireless devices can now put it all into the hands of every individual. This is quite real already and will become the mainstay of knowledge access very soon.

What can now happen is that divergence will be wireless. That is already true for radio and television. You do not plug your radio into a wire to get a signal, although you can receive your television signal over a cable as well as through its rabbit ears. A broadcast news team converges aspects of a news event, from around town or around the world, into a studio and out through a transmitter that sends a signal over a radiant frequency. The divergence is achieved as the news is picked up by individual radios and television sets tuned to the transmitter's frequency. The Internet, too, can be broadcast into radiant frequencies so that it can be tuned in by individuals. What Steve Jobs demonstrated with the iMac and hoola hoop was exactly that. He was holding a wireless device in his hands that could receive the Internet, and all that it contains, as it was broadcast by a nearby transmitter. The user of the wireless device not only receives the Internet but can communicate wirelessly back into the Internet.

The telegraph is one-way in real time. One person taps out a message that another person receives at the other end. The person at the other end must wait until the message is received before he can tap back a response. The telephone is two-way in real time. When she and he are connected through telephones, they can speak and hear back and forth, or both speak and hear at once. Radio and television are one-way wireless transmissions in real time. The listener and viewer receive a signal but cannot respond. The wired Internet does all of the above, with the significant advantage of not being trapped in real time. The ephemeral radio message or television show appears at a certain time, runs its course, and disappears. The ten o'clock news is over at 10:30 and has vanished into the mystery of the time dimension. The Internet is there all the time—twenty-four hours a day, seven days a week. Although Internet broadcasts are originally streamed at a time specific, they also stream into the memory in a server somewhere (or on your hard drive, if you so choose). The telephone made a step into the hypercommunications arena when the conference call became possible, where several people can take part in a phone call simultaneously. The Internet is a conference call with everybody on the planet who has Internet access. The wiring is there for that and is being used by millions of people every day.

There is no technical difference between what the wireless Internet devices are capturing and what is delivered over a wire to bring the Internet into a computer. What Steve Jobs had in his hands and was passing through the hoola hoop was the entire Internet. All the wireless device has to capture is zeros and ones—the same zeros and ones that would have arrived in the computer from the Internet over a telephone or cable wire. Computers tied down by wires for uses such as educational Internet resources will surely become as obsolete as the SR-71.

Computers are cumbersome hardware in the classroom setting, not like the good old days when students had individual tablets, and the teacher could write on the chalkboard. Even better days are coming in silicon and radiance. For now, the classroom hardware hurdles are several and high. You must have computers. You must know how to use the computers. You must have the know-how to fix them when there are problems. You have to have an Internet connection to plug into. Then you bring in the kids. You now need enough computers to go around.

If the computers are sitting on the kids' desks, you cannot see what a student is doing without walking around and standing over his or her shoulder. You must be able to enforce class discipline when many or all of the kids cannot be seen from the front of the room because they are sitting behind the computers.

All of these problems are being addressed in the several-year-old crusade to wire the schools. Much has been achieved, but new problems come along with the achievements. Computer classrooms must continuously be updated or they slip toward obsolescence. Many computers contributed to schools are too old to be very useful. As the Internet gets richer, slower modems in many schools become less and less adequate. I was at a meeting of high school teachers who were trying to get up to speed as technology coordinators. They shared their frustrations and horror stories about not being able to keep machines online or explain them to teachers. A fellow in the back of the room finally stood up and said, "Let the kids do it." He described a team of students he had put together in his high school to keep the computers and wiring working. The rest of the meeting consisted of getting his advice on how to organize a tech team of kids for a high school.

When students study at home, there is another set of problems. For starters, when a student is using the Internet to do homework in a house with just one telephone line, the telephone is busy, and other family members cannot make or receive phone calls. Just one computer in a home is a problem when there are several brothers and sisters with homework to do. Does he get to do research on the Internet when she needs to type her book report?

Good hardware solutions for schools and homes have steadily come on the scene. I visited a fifth-grade classroom in New Jersey where the computers had been placed under transparent flat tables. The students sat comfortably behind the tables in full view of the teacher, as they looked through the tabletops at their monitor screens and reached under the edge of the table in front of them to type on their keyboards. Many of the problems for classroom management had disappeared. A projection unit at the front of the classroom allowed the teacher to display pages from the Internet in view of all the students. Internet cable connections and cheap second telephone lines for homes are increasingly available, and there are new call-waiting alert systems for households online.

Every problem I have been mentioning will shrink and begin to disappear the day that, figuratively, Steve Jobs hands tomorrow's iBooks to students. I am not promoting Apple's iBook. In coming months, as the wireless Internet becomes available, there will be many vendors and many variations of handheld Internet access devices. The back-to-school tradition of buying paper tablets could even disappear entirely. The tablet will be replaced by an inexpensive computer that is the student's personal possession. He will use it for reading, writing, and arithmetic. From it he can connect to everything that is known. He will record and store his notes and make his portfolios within it. He will toss it in his backpack and use it both at school and at home. If he breaks it, loses it, or wants a later model, it can be easily discarded and replaced by another one. He will never lose his data, because he will have it stored online in another safe server, probably where his Web site is located. He will use it to exchange classwork and homework with his teacher through her handheld computer. None of the above will require connection at any time to wires. It all will be taking place in the radiant medium.

Imagine what a future student computer tablet might be like. Perhaps it would have the shape and dimensions of standard 8.5-by-11-inch letter-size paper and would be one inch thick. It would be hinged along one long end and open up like the iBook or any other laptop computer. A monitor screen would fill up half of the opened device. The other half would have a keyboard for typing, a calculator keypad, and a space for drawing, like a palm device has. The screen could be detachable along the hinged side for use as an e-book. The texts of entire books could be downloaded from the Internet into the detachable screen's memory. The reading screen could be held by a student in her hands or set on a rack. A tiny detachable remote controller could point to the screen and virtually turn pages, scroll, and otherwise move around in the text. The e-tablet would be able to beam pages wirelessly to a printer. A scanner stick could be pulled out from a slot and passed over print or images to import them into the computer. The entire device would require little computer memory because the student's resources and original work would be stored somewhere in cyberspace on a large server computer and accessed on demand by the device in the student's hand or by any other computer where the student might be working. The device would also be a telephone, radio, television, and camera.

Merriam-Webster's tells us that the word *antenna* was coined in 1646 to mean "one of a pair of slender movable segmented sensory organs on the head of insects, myriapods, and crustaceans." The second meaning given is "a usually metallic device (as a rod or wire) for radiating or receiving radio waves."[3] A student's wireless tablet is very much like a sensory organ for receiving ideas that can be radiated to her from all over the world. Antennas that radiate the Internet make it possible to use wireless student tablets instead of stationary, plugged-in computers in schools. The timing for the final step in the completion of the Great Change reminds me of the old story about William the Conqueror. Having spent a long season on the coast of Normandy directing the building of hundreds of boats, the morning came when he was to lead his mighty flotilla into the channel for the crossing to attack England. King William's fine boat was faster than the rest. He set sail in the dark hours before dawn. When there was enough light to see the horizon toward France, it was vacant. His mighty fleet was not to be seen. The king ordered his crew to haul down the sails and serve him his breakfast. When they had set the food on the royal table, he sat down before the fare to eat. By the time he finished his meal, the eastern horizon was crowded by a forest of masts sticking into the sky. Fair winds and William's optimism led the Normans forward across the water to a successful landing and the conquest of England.

A forest of radiant antennas advances on our horizon. There is no particular William waiting to lead the radiant conquest, but his sort of optimism is helping to compel the advance. A few weeks after the lesson I learned from Steve Jobs, I got another dose of wireless basics from Dr. Irving S. Hamer. He is one of the seven members of the New York City Board of Education, which runs the largest school system in the world. I was presenting a seminar at the Manhattan High Schools Annual Technology Conference. Dr. Hamer spoke at the convocation of the conference the day before the seminars, addressing three hundred high school teachers, school board representatives, Manhattan District staff, and business supporters and partners of public schools. He spoke of the many frustrations, delays, and seemingly unsolvable problems that exist in bringing computers online in the New York City public schools so that students can use and benefit from the technology. He then focused his optimism on wireless computers for students.

Dr. Hamer said that a technology committee he headed within the Board of Education would recommend in September 2000 that the New York City public schools become wireless and that the following September the board provide all of the system's 73,000 fourth graders with laptop computers of their own. Each year thereafter, all children entering the fourth grade would receive laptops. When I realized that the way to solve the problems related to wiring the schools was not to solve them, I was elated. There is a better way: go wireless. I became a believer on the spot. I do not know if the New York schools will implement the leadership that Dr. Hamer outlined. But I feel certain that providing ways for students to do classwork and research without wires is a shift that will untangle and snip many of the woes of wiring. The handle of the digital sword that will cut the Gordian knot of education woes is wireless computing. It swings the blade of the Grand Idea.

Whatever exact form handheld wireless tablets do take, they will flip-flop how student access to computers is measured. That measurement up until now has been taken by counting the number of kids crowded around computers sitting on desks and wired to data cables. As the Software and Information Industry Association reports, there is progress: "The recent dramatic change in access is evident by the 31% increase between 1998 and 1999 in students per Internet-access computer from 19.7:1 to 13.6:1. While great progress is being made, efforts are needed to better integrate Internet technology into teaching and learning, thereby leveraging its full potential." [4] What I learned from Dr. Hamer was that by cutting the cord in the classroom from the computer to the dataport, the measure no longer need be how many kids share computers, but how many students possess computers. As children, my generation gathered with our families around console radios in our living rooms, and later around the televisions that replaced radios as sources of news and entertainment. Transistor radios, and then portable disc-players, became the private appliances of the generations that followed mine. For many of the Generation Now children, the cell phone has already become a personal appliance. This wireless telephone will quickly evolve into a handheld device empowering students to interact with everything that is known.

This change is coming because everything in the digital soup can be transmitted wirelessly. Wireless digital communication is simply broadcasting zeros and ones on one of the wavelengths across the electromagnetic radiation spectrum. The signal that streams the zeros and ones can be broadcast along a radiant frequency from a satellite, sent through copper wire or optical cable, or manually tapped on the wall to be heard next door. In whatever medium it travels, the code is binary, with just two possible signals.

The forest of radiant antennas entering our horizon vary in size and power. A data cable installer explained a job that she had recently worked on as building an upside-down tree of copper wire inside a building. She had been part of the team that installed cable for wireless reception in Rockefeller Center. It was all copper, not optical, she explained. Optical cable, which carries visible frequencies of light, is proving better for some applications, and copper for others. For years, the digital signal was carried over wires in analog format with a device at the sending end to turn digital into analog and a device called a modem at the receiving end to turn the analog signal back to digital so that the receiving computer could understand it. In each of these situations, you had to plug a wire from your computer into a jack to receive the data signal.

The installer told me that there is a big antenna on top of the building she worked on at Rockefeller Center. Then there is a main big fat copper cable that extends down from the rooftop receiver through the center of the building. From the central trunk smaller copper cables branch out through the floors. Every so often down the branches of the cables, little antennas stick out from the copper broadcasting the signal captured on the roof and sent down the trunk. Of course, at this stage of the crossing from hardwire to wireless, the main usage of the upside-down copper tree in the building is by people with cell phones. Even in their present state as cell phones, these handheld devices are showing up in classrooms. In Nordic countries, where a high percentage of kids have their own cell phones, they have been doing things like sending each other answers to test questions across their classroom. One kid bounces her signal wirelessly into the radiant medium and back into the classroom to a friend on the other side of the room. This questionable practice is not the most auspicious introduction of wirelessness to education, but it demonstrates the revolutionary new mobility of ideas.

The cell phone industry is pioneering wireless signaling and building an infrastructure that I expect will evolve into the backbone of the wireless Internet. Certainly it will be a long time, if ever, before all copper and optical cable are replaced by wireless radiation of the Internet. What I have been describing is not intended as a technical opus. It is background for my prediction that handheld wireless devices for students will mitigate and then close the digital divide both in the United States and around the world. The saddest problem with wiring the schools and getting students online was not mentioned above: the intractable difficulty of preventing a digital divide. A study released by the U.S. Department of Education in August 2000 reported bad news, as described in the *New York Times:*

> Almost half the money from federal education programs is going to the poorest schools in the country, but those schools continue to lack qualified teachers and technological resources, including computers with Internet access. . . . The report confirmed the existence of a growing digital divide in the country's classrooms, which keeps students from low-income families from having access to computers and the Internet. While federal money paid for almost a quarter of the computers that schools received in the 1997–1998 school year, "high-poverty schools had less access to technology than low-poverty schools in terms of the quantity, quality and connectivity of computers," the report said.[5]

When all children are empowered with their own handheld computer devices that are as inexpensive as telephones, the digital divide will disappear. The infrastructure for transmitting the Internet signal into schools and homes is a factor. Great savings in money and effort will result from not trying to equip classrooms with computers and having to maintain them, along with their wiring. Perhaps upside-down copper trees will need to be added to big school buildings. Students in impoverished areas may at first have to take their handheld tablets to a community center where transmitters are radiating. But these challenges are no more difficult nor any larger than those that successfully brought radio and television to everyone. Like Johnny Appleseed, the cell phone industry is very busy scattering the forests of antennas.

Is it faith or fantasy to predict that the poor and even the poorest children will actually get the handheld wireless tablets? A pivotal factor makes it inevitable that they will: the need to be met will no longer be to provide classrooms for them where they share computers that are wired down. The digital divide is defined by some classrooms having more computers than other classrooms. Because of wiring needs, capital investments in computers, maintenance requirements, and quick obsolescence, equality has eluded us. The new measure will not be about classrooms, but about kids: how many students have handheld wireless computers? As the price plummets, the kids will all get the devices. Children of poverty lack very many things, but few of them do not have cheap radios. The telephone and television technologies have found their way into almost all of the poorest and most remote places in America where children dwell, because these technologies have become very cheap and people want them. The handheld wireless tablet can find its way into the hands of all children for the same reasons. And let us not linger over the absurdity that, once a way to end the digital divide is available, the money will not rush in from many sources to provide inexpensive wireless devices for all children.

The wireless world is not a distant dream. It is coming fast, certainly, in the business arena. The META Group and the Digital Consulting Group sponsored a summit on wireless computing in September 2000. The cover of the conference schedule announced: "By 2003, half of all business users will be mobile, and each will typically use three to four different information appliances, seamlessly connected via Personal Area Networks to enterprise applications and the Internet." [6] Although technical and business seminars dominated this summit schedule, there was one presentation by a university. There are experiments in place with antennas planted around campuses so that the student has wireless access in every building, and outdoors as well. The forest of antennas is appearing over the horizon of education.

Of course, the coming of cheaper wireless handheld student tablets will not directly cure other problems with the schools, like another one pointed out in the previous *New York Times* article:

> One of the report's most disturbing findings showed that teachers' aides rather than qualified teachers were teaching many students in Title I schools. Although almost all of the teachers' aides in Title I had a high school diploma, only 19 percent had a bachelor's degree. . . . Half of the instructional workers supported by Title I money were teachers' aides. But 41 percent of these aides said that they spent at least half of their time teaching students on their own, without a teacher present.[7]

But there is cause for optimism here in the lessening need to hardwire the schools. Wireless access to the Internet should be a big help with the challenges surrounding the development of twenty-first-century teachers, because, for one thing, money can be reallotted from wiring schools and buying expensive computers to meeting other school needs. When we reach the day that every student and teacher has a handheld computer priced, say, under $50, a weight of frustration and depression will be lifted from those who do the diligent and sometimes tragic duty of teaching in bad schools. In the mid–nineteenth century, when Horace Mann was envisioning universal public education, hardware was not a big deal. A blackboard, some chalk, paper, pencils, quill pens, and ink just about did it. Schools could be established in teeming ghettos and wild western towns with no more than those tools, and a teacher, a room and some chairs, and maybe a school bell. Even books were not much of a problem, because nobody had very many. Public libraries developed and high school libraries followed, but children were not exposed to a wide range of reading.

The digital divide has occurred as some schools have acquired computer technology and others have not. The once simple world of school hardware has become a fiscal nightmare. The schools left out of the loop have become less and less tolerable places to teach. It is not just lack of money that causes the absence of teachers from these schools. In working with dozens of schools operating below expected levels, I have met incredibly bright, dedicated, and able teachers. One friend of mine, who has a doctoral degree, left college teaching eight years ago to become a kindergarten teacher in a school with many problems. She says that if she can have kids for a year, she can teach them to read, and then "they will make it." There are many teachers and principals who have worked heroically in difficult schools and simply burned out. They get great credit, but things should not be that difficult. I predict that wireless handheld computers that include Internet access will make teaching in now difficult schools less frustrating and more fun. The kids will respond to having their own tools, just as ghetto kids did a century and a half ago to learning their letters by writing them on a tablet. The optimism of kids is the elixir that will restore the good health of teaching in America.

The wireless empowerment to knowledge will occur not only in the United States. All over the planet people will have increasing access to the Internet as the radiant medium becomes wireless. For now, the digital divide is worldwide, and efforts are being made elsewhere to connect children to the Internet so that they can learn. Bernard Krishner, a former journalist, has successfully established an Internet connection through Thailand's Shin Satellite to a school attended by four hundred young children in the remote cluster of villages of Robib in rural Cambodia. In the same vein, a *New York Times* story in May 2000 described a temple in Embalam, India, where two solar-powered computers are operated by villagers. The article comments:

> At a time of growing unease about the global gap between technology knows and know-nots, India is fast becoming a laboratory for small experiments like the one at the temple that aim to link isolated rural pockets to the borderless world of knowledge. Local governments and nonprofit groups are testing new approaches to provide villages where barely anyone can afford a telephone with computer centers that are accessible to all.[8]

Another *New York Times* story from India is instructive:

> Bombay, Aug. 29, 2000—Maqbool Ahmed has dreams of instant wealth, which ordinarily would require a mighty burst of imagination from a man living in the Bombay slum of Geeta Nagar, a hideous warren of hovels where the air reeks of kerosene and fish, and there are only 24 toilets for 6,000 people. But come 9 p.m., Mondays through Thursdays, Mr. Ahmed, like virtually everyone else in this monsoon-swamped ghetto, ignores the leaky roof, turns on a cheap black-and-white television and watches the Indian version of *Who Wants to Be a Millionaire.*[9]

There are only twenty-four toilets for six thousand people, yet virtually everyone watches a television program! Surely, the television signal is not wired into the black-and-white sets in Maqbool, but arrives on radiated frequencies through rabbit ears. The wireless Internet will soon be as easily available as "Who Wants to Be a Millionaire." Cynics may think that a place where television sets are more numerous than toilets might not be interested in self-improvement. But then, why do they watch the show? The digital divide has occurred not because people do not want their children to learn, but because the hardware has been too cumbersome and expensive.

As Steve Jobs demonstrated in the new iBook, when Internet access marries the convenience and ubiquity of cell phones, education will become wireless. Thailand's Shin Satellite will beam knowledge from the radiance directly into the handheld tablet devices of the children of Robib. The kids in Nordic classes will receive the Internet as well as messages from each other. If Marvin Hamer has his way, the 73,000 new fourth graders in New York City will connect to the radiance each year. The last barrier to getting knowledge to the students will go away. George Gilder, my third teacher on the subject of wirelessness, describes the radiant medium in the following passage. I would make no effort to compete in describing his gorgeous vision:

> Imagine gazing at the web from far in space. To you, peering through your spectroscope, mapping the mazes of electromagnetism in its path, the Web appears as a global efflorescence, a resonant sphere of light. It is the physical phase space of the telecosm, the radiant chrysalis from which will spring a new global economy.
>
> The luminous ball reflects Maxwell's rainbow, with each arc of light bearing a signatory wavelength. As the mass of the traffic flows through fiber-optic trunks, it glows infrared, with the network backbones looming as focused beams of 1550-nanometer radiance running across continents and under the seas. As more and more people use wireless means to access the Net, this infrared ball grows a penumbra of microwaves, suffused with billions of moving sparks from multimegahertz teleputers or digital cellular phones. Piercing through the penumbra are rich spikes of radio frequencies confined in the coaxial cables circling through neighborhoods and hooking to each household. Spangling the Net are more than 100 million nodes of concentrated standing waves, each an Internet host, a computer with a microprocessor running at a microwave frequency from the hundreds of megahertz to the gigahertz. The radiance reaches upward between 400 and 800 miles to thousands of low-orbit satellites, each sending forth cords of "light" between Earth and sky in the Ku band between 12 and 18 gigahertz.[10]

It is a joyous thing to think about enlightenment traveling on highways and byways of radiant frequencies from everyone to everyone. In the final chapter, I describe the hyperformations that knowledge is taking in the environment depicted by Gilder. As we go to that discussion it is important to note that, for all its beauty, the radiance described above is nothing more than a communications system. It is like our physical brain and not like our mind. It transports commerce, it is not commerce itself. For education, the radiance is where students and teachers go for knowledge to learn and teach. The Great Change will be complete when a student can hold in his or her hands everything that is known.

NOTES

1. Richard Parkinson, *Cracking Codes: The Rosetta Stone and Deciphermen* (Berkeley: University of California Press, 1999), 14.

2. Parkinson, *Cracking Codes,* 14.

3. *Merriam-Webster's Collegiate Dictionary,* 10th ed., 1997.

4. Software and Information Association, "Trends Shaping the Digital Economy," <http://www.trendsreport.net/education/2.html>, August 2000 [accessed 23 October 2000].

5. Edward Wong, "Poorest Schools Lack Teachers and Computers," *New York Times,* 13 August 2000.

6. Summit on Wireless Computing, Orlando, Florida, 12–14 September 2000. Sponsored by Digital Consulting Institute, www.dci.com and META Group, www.metagroup.com.

7. Summit on Wireless Computing, 12–14 September 2000

8. John Markoff, "Connecting Rural India to the World," *New York Times,* 28 May 2000.

9. Barry Bearak, "Many, Many in India Want to Be a Millionaire," *New York Times,* 30 August 2000.

10. George Gilder, *Forbes ASAP* <http://www.discovery.org/viewDB/index.php3?program=George%20Gilder%20Archives&command=view&id=14>, 1 October 1999 [accessed 13 August 2000].

IV

THE GOLDEN HORIZON

The glory that was Greece, the ghost of the library of Alexandria, the magnificence of the Renaissance were each goldened by knowledge. The radiance now dawning conveys a broad spectrum of information, its most important portion being the rays of gold flowing within the mighty web and placed in the hands of anyone who tunes in. Elegantly entwined, like thinking itself, the golden radiation of knowledge is the Grand Idea.

10

The Grand Idea

The summer after two of my nephews graduated from high school they visited me for a long weekend. Sons of my two brothers, the cousins are one month apart in age, became fraternity brothers at New Mexico State University, and are great friends. Both guys are over six-foot-four, and when I introduced them to friends the night we attended the ballet at Lincoln Center, I called them "my protection." They arrived in New York City full of merriment, and we had a wonderful time. I managed to borrow a weekend cottage in the Hamptons and a car. One nephew owned a truck and the other a small sports car. They had been driving around West Texas and New Mexico since getting their driver's licenses at age sixteen. Seeking to keep harmony, I proposed that for the trip to the Hamptons, one would be the driver on the way out and the other on the way back. They immediately demonstrated their reaction to New York traffic during their taxi ride from La Guardia Airport to my apartment by saying, "You drive."

I drove as one nephew manned the maps and the other the radio and air conditioning. The weekend cottage was quite fine, complete with a swimming pool and sprinklers that turned on automatically in the middle of the night to ensure that the plants in the yard, collected from several countries, were kept healthy. We visited the beach, using the resident's pass I was loaned along with the cottage. It was all quite wonderful. As we drove around enjoying the sights, we paused at the driveways leading into expansive estates surrounded by high hedges and landscaped to form lovely settings for great houses. Some of the estates were old, built by robber barons and once frequented by the F. Scott Fitzgerald crowd. There were new ones as well, built by some of the most financially successful people of the later twentieth century. As my nephews and I discussed what we were seeing, we realized that few places on Earth have such lavish dwellings. One of the guys commented that he had seen neighborhoods like that in areas around Los Angeles. My nephews began keeping count of the Jaguars, Ferraris, and Lamborghinis that rolled past us as we cruised around the Hamptons. No feature of these most extravagant cars was lost on the guys. We came to decide that what we were seeing was life in the grand style.

How is the Internet a grand idea for education? In the remaining pages I use some definitions of grand to imply how its several rich and lofty nuances may apply to our coming wireless age for learning and schools. We begin by looking beyond our current frustrations in using the Internet and at the powerful dimensions of its new interconnectedness.

The Internet seems like such a mess to most people these days. You have to get a computer, figure out how to make it respond, get a wire at the back of it plugged into something that leads to the Internet. Then what? E-mail is pretty easy to figure out, and using it quickly becomes a habit. Other things people figure out to do on the Internet are almost completely driven by individual needs and projects: trading stock, buying books, scheduling trips and buying tickets, finding suppliers for a particular business, and sharing family pictures. In all of that apparent fragmentation, how could there be cohesiveness on a large scale?

The fact of the matter is that interconnectedness is inherent in the Internet; we just do not yet see it. From the beginning, the online system was set up to overcome the fragmentation of information that has plagued humankind since we walked out of the garden of our origins. The inventor of the World Wide Web, Tim Berners-Lee, explains:

> What the first bit of [coding] led me to was . . . a vision encompassing the decentralized, organic growth of ideas, technology, and society. It is a vision that provides us with new freedom, and allows us to grow faster than we ever could when we were fettered by the hierarchical classification systems into which we bound ourselves. It leaves the entirety of our previous ways of working as just one tool among many. . . . It brings the workings of society closer to the working of our mind.[1]

The Grand Idea is the sum total of the organic growth of ideas. The meaning of the word *grand* includes all the notions that define the Grand Idea. *Merriam-Webster's* definition of grand includes:

> having more importance than others: FOREMOST
> having higher rank than others bearing the same general designation
> INCLUSIVE, COMPRESHENSIVE
> DEFINITIVE, INCONTROVERTIBLE
> CHIEF, PRINCIPAL
> large and striking in size, scope, extent, or conception
> LAVISH, SUMPTUOUS
> marked by a regal form and dignity
> fine or imposing in appearance or impression
> LOFTY, SUBLIME[2]

Life in the Hamptons is grand because it is lavish, sumptuous, regal, and dignified. Its estates and automobiles are large and striking in scope, extent, or conception.

The life led is considered by its participants to be lofty and sublime, as they strive to be fine or imposing in appearance or impression. A grand slam in bridge or baseball earns its label by being comprehensive, definitive, and incontrovertible. A grand marshal is the chief of something, having higher rank than others bearing the designation *marshal* alone. A grand master is the foremost player.

The sum total of what I know is my personal grand idea because it is large and comprehensive for me. It began to connect within my mind more than sixty years ago, and it has grown richer with every new tidbit I have learned and every new idea that has sprung from connecting some of the tidbits. I know how arithmetic works, and thousands upon thousands of words have entered my mind and woven their meaning into the fabric of my thought. History has been a mental labor of love, hanging new characters and events on a broadening, thickening chronology spreading into what I know about political theory, the growth of science, the evolution of ideas, and expression through the arts. What I know is not a bunch of separate things. It has become large and striking in size, scope, extent, and conception. It is all one interconnected web that is inclusive and comprehensive within my mind.

There are aspects of being human that are distinct from and more fundamental and critical than what we know, I suppose, but these can be refined and supported by what we know. Nurture and acculturation go hand in hand with learning knowledge, but they are not the same thing. Every living thing must preserve its life and achieve prosperity. Plants do that and know nothing in the way our minds know, since they have no brains to house minds. There have been two squirrels in my backyard that knew they could carry two peanuts at a time. At some point in the scale of complexity of the animal mind, primitive knowing begins. Like squirrels, humans seem to possess certain innate knowledge that comes with the territory of being alive.

My grand idea is more than innate knowledge rationed to me by my human DNA. It is an edifice I have woven in my mind by learning and thinking. It is something I have built and something I use. It has and continues to grow organically. Beyond love and survival, it is of foremost importance to me. I wish it were more lavish and sumptuous, and I continue to work to make it so. Enjoying what I know is among the most lofty and sublime aspects of living.

Until the Internet came along, there was no conceivable way of weaving a grand idea outside of an individual mind—except by doing so in other minds, and that is called teaching. Of course we teach our children not to hit each other, how to safely cross the street, and many other lessons mama squirrel teaches her babies. And we teach the highest lessons of love. But we begin early as well, to teach the colors, and words, and numbers, and then the great stories, fascinating sciences, promising technologies, and everything else we can muster on our own from the enormous sum of what is now known by humankind.

The Great Change has made it inevitable that the Grand Idea would be woven within the Internet, just as my own grand idea arose in my mind. How could that possibly be happening in that messy maze we encounter when we log on to the Internet? The Internet has millions and millions of pages, most designed locally and thrown out into cyberspace. Beautiful as George Gilder's description of it may be, it is enormously complex, and the radiance he describes is an organic communication system, not an idea. The fact is that the Internet's complexity is what allows it to contain the Grand Idea. The Internet is complex, in a primitive way as the brain is complex. The more vast the Internet grows, the more suited it becomes to house the Grand Idea. The most vast and complex known entity is the human brain. The most vast and complex communications system ever created is the Internet.

I have written this book to share the most fascinating experience of my life: spending four years immersed in the formation of the Grand Idea. The steps I have written about have occurred to me as I witnessed a reality concealed from most by the technical hurdles imposed by the infant Internet. My perception of an idea as being a connection of scraps of thought came several years ago from studying theories of brain function. The failures of predigital communication contrast with the new opportunities presented by nonlinear, organic digital memory and media. The reduction of everything known to a single code of zeros and ones long ago struck me as a gee-whiz good idea. The notion of a digital soup of all the zeros and ones reminded me of how everything I know is etched in my brain and how I can manipulate it by opening and closing synaptic gates. The powerful synergy of everything reduced to one code that could then be interrelated in dimensionless ways struck me with awe. And then all of this, almost suddenly, is dumped into a wired, and soon to become radiant, communication system that connects everyone to everyone else dimensionlessly. What more could happen?

Much more had to happen. The potentials opened up by the Internet are huge. Pornography has never had it so good. But prostitutes have always taken advantage of the loose rules along frontiers. Like every great exploration and migration, ships have been launched and lost. Great fortunes have been made. Young adventurers and bored executives have grabbed the day. Also, as is ever the case in discovering new ground, it is taking a while to understand its greater value.

Substances that sit within the Internet are hyperwebs. Like my family Web site, their parts are interconnected in multiple dimensions; they are hyperlinked. When scraps of thought within my mind become related, they are interconnected in a similar way, and once they shift to become comprehensible, they are an idea that I have in my mind. The digital medium is the first one we have invented that can mirror the hyperconnections of my bits of thought as they occur in my mind. The Internet is a digital medium and mirror for hyperwebs on the grandest of scales. Just imagine what could happen if all the people in the world who have ever lived contributed what they knew into the Internet. Do not imagine: watch. Exactly that is happening.

For starters, the Internet contains: the Bible in every old and new translation; the current theories and ongoing DNA and linguistic research on the emergence of *homo sapiens* from Africa or elsewhere; the Web site of the Somerset Level where the Sweet Track ran; ancient and current speculation on what happened at Atlantis, including some satellite images of possible Atlantis sites; the home page of the tomb built for Emperor Qin Shi Haung; everything written by Aristotle,

Buddha, Confucius, and Pericles (and everything we still have that was written by Herodotus and all other writers during the Golden Age of Greece); everything left from the collections at the library at Alexandria, and most of the books collected for the New York City libraries by John Jacob Astor, James Lenox, and Samuel J. Tilden; the Koran and related literature; the works of Donatello; the complete symphonies and other compositions of the classical composers; and so on and on. As described earlier, there is a great deal of knowledge that exists only on the Internet. It includes active science, genetics, space exploration, medicine, ecology, animal migrations, archaeology, and so on and on. Current affairs take place increasingly on the Internet with updates on legislation, current information posted on country Web sites, and news reports moving into Web sites and remaining there for reference and study. More and more Web pages are being specifically constructed to retain and impart knowledge. National scientific laboratories display tutorials about their projects, museums showcase their collections, and businesses add background about what they make and sell, and so on and on.

Can it be that something coherent can rise out of this brain dump into cyberspace? Because of the organic structure of the World Wide Web, planned from the beginning by Tim Berners-Lee, it is inevitable that not only coherence but elegance is emerging. It will do so for the same reasons that you and I cause a grand idea of our own to grow over our lifetime of learning and thinking—and because any idea is sublimely elegant. We shall cherish and nurture the Grand Idea for the same reason we still wince when we think of the fires at the library of Alexandria.

The Grand Idea is a hyperweb within the communications hyperweb of the Internet. The Grand Idea is not a part of the Internet; it is a set of connections among scraps of digital memory. What is within the scraps of memory are pieces of knowledge, ranging from Aristotle's *Rhetoric* to the latest image captured by the Hubble Space Telescope. The Grand Idea is the set of connections, just like an infant's concept of a tree is a set of connections among tall things, leaves, things that make shade, and things colored green. When the baby connects things that are wheels to this pattern of connections, the hyperweb she is building is not a good idea. She has to disconnect the wheel notion. As soon as Internet users started making their own pages, they spontaneously began connecting to their favorite links and listing them to share with people visiting their pages. This habit began the formation of the Grand Idea. When somebody lists their favorite pornography links, they are definitely not taking part in building the Grand Idea. When I list all of my cousins' pages on my family Web site, I am not building the Grand Idea. But when a medievalist lists his favorite castle links, he has created a small hyperweb for the study of history, and it has become part of the infancy of the Grand Idea. Because he is knowledgeable about castles, he will not link to information that is wrong. He will link to the Web pages having more importance than most, the foremost sources.

The hyperwebbing of knowledge has been undertaken in numerous fields on a larger scale. You can revisit the Archaic and Classical world of the West at the Perseus Project.[3] Among many other things you will find are the full texts of the

Golden Age Greek writers, in Greek and in English. The inclusive, comprehensive, definitive grand goals of this project are set out on its Web site:

What is the Perseus Project?

The Perseus Project is an evolving digital library of resources for the study of the ancient world and beyond. Collaborators initially formed the project to construct a large, heterogeneous collection of materials, textual and visual, on the Archaic and Classical Greek world. Planning for Perseus began in 1985; the project was formally established in July, 1987. Since then, the Perseus Project has published two CD-ROMs and created the on-line Perseus Digital Library. Recent expansion into Latin texts and tools and Renaissance materials has served to add more coverage within Perseus and has prompted the project to explore new ways of presenting complex resources for electronic publication.

Goals and Mission

Our primary goal is to bring a wide range of source materials to as large an audience as possible. We anticipate that greater accessibility to the sources for the study of the humanities will strengthen the quality of questions, lead to new avenues of research, and connect more people through the connection of ideas. Although members of the project have collected a large set of core data (roughly 225 gigabytes, at this writing), a good deal of the work done at the project focuses on how best to structure the framework for the massive set of texts, images, plans, and maps which comprise the library. In addition to gathering more materials, we continue to build and supplement our powerful set of searching and indexing tools. These tools are at the heart of our work: they form the connections between the various kinds of materials within Perseus and facilitate the exploration of these materials for general readers and specialists alike.

The Perseus Project, like the brain, converges and diverges. There are many nodes of convergence on the Web pages, and what is learned diverges out to people across the Internet.

Hot topics in science, such as genetics, have competitive reporting Web sites that are jockeying for position as the chief, principle, incontrovertible hyperwebs of in-depth and current knowledge. Imagine what it might have been like if Archimedes put up a hot topics Web site. He virtually has. There are several excellent Web sites about Archimedes, including a fine one from Drexel University.[4] It includes illustrations and animations from a September 2000 British Broadcasting Corporation (BBC) documentary about the attempted reconstruction of the ancient technologist's terrifying war machine. Another page provides the legendary last words of Archimedes in Greek, Latin, and English: "Don't disturb my circles." An audio clip lets you hear his words in Greek.

The great twentieth-century physicist Stephen Hawking has created a Web site. It offers a memoir, "A Brief History of Mine," that begins: "Stephen William Hawking was born on 8 January 1942 (300 years after the death of Galileo) in Oxford, England." Click the icon next to Does God play dice? to choose from Public Lectures or Physical Colloquiums. The latter group begins with the caution: "These lectures assume a level of Physics which is of at least at University Degree level." [5]

Dispel any apprehension that the Grand Idea will be riddled with junk or descend to the mediocre. The hyperweb of the Grand Idea is being woven by the people who know the most of the fabric of the collected knowledge of humankind and leading the advances being made into knowledge that is new. For the same reason the infant rejects the wheel to grasp the idea of a tree, both the builders and users of the Grand Idea are rejecting inferior Web pages. The medievalist, the Perseus people, the Archimedes scholars at Drexel, and Professor Hawking are the foremost judges in their fields of what to include in the Grand Idea. As cute as a third grader's Web page about castles may be, it will not pass muster. The child's page is part of her immature building process toward what she will know over her life within her mind. It is not properly linked to the definitive and sublime Grand Idea of what is known by humankind. And it is not just the academics who are keeping the Grand Idea pure as it grows. Everyone who accesses knowledge pages is helping. Search technology has emerged so that Web sites are ranked by how often they are visited. This method quickly determines that more students are using the medievalist's page about castles than are stopping by to study the page on the subject by the third grader.

The fundamental free-arena nature of the Internet will also operate to keep the Grand Idea from being corrupted. Competition sharpens the market for quality. An exciting new way for colleges and universities to compete for students is the reposting of knowledge-laden Web pages. Many institutions of higher learning already do this in Web projects ranging from individual lectures and illustrations by professors to elaborate departmental exhibits of ongoing research. The emergence of pages from the academy is a new, unsolicited, high-quality resource for the schools for which they do not have to pay. As their use by middle and high school students becomes more widespread, the impact on campus recruiting is inevitable. The campus with the best virtual chemistry pages is bound to attract the attention of future chemistry majors who are making college decisions. An interesting trend is under way as colleges and universities develop specialized Web presences for biology, artificial intelligence, rhetoric, law, agriculture, history, and many other academic fields. The unstated goal is apparent: to become the definitive, incontrovertible, chief, principal Web source in a field, and to be large and striking in size, scope, extent, and conception. This is a grand goal and will engage great students in their respective specialties.

Competition has a potential role in corporate Web sites, and I am hopeful that a small trend now under way will take off and become standard practice. Large business Web sites have huge budgets. Education and the corporation benefit when a small amount of the cost of the site is devoted to knowledge pages. It is a very simple idea: the corporation explains what it makes or does. There are already many examples of this process. A fine one is the Intel Museum, which offers exhibits with text and animation explaining how chips are made, how microprocessors work, the history of the microprocessor, clean rooms, how transistors work, and memory technology.[6] It is a fabulous hyperweb of knowledge about digital technology, and it connects readily into the Grand Idea. It will be a wonderful source of lavish, sumptuous, fine, and imposing-in-appearance knowledge Web pages if deep-pocketed corporations move into an unspoken competition to create sites that kids will use in school. If you are in a position to nudge action in this direction at your company, I urge you to do so. I remember the resolve of corporations and businesses in the 1980s to partner with schools to improve education. Some good work was done, but there were frustrations, too. Adding quality knowledge Web pages to corporate and business sites is an immediate way to help a wide sweep of students, teachers, and schools. The public relations value is not lost on me. But I know firsthand of the sincerity of the motivations of corporate leaders, like everybody else, to want to help kids learn. This is a way to do just that.

There are many other kinds of Web sites that are including hyperwebbed knowledge pages that will connect to the Grand Idea. Among the groups I have wandered through are cattle breeders and labor unions. In both cases, about half of the organizations had some hyperlinked pages devoted to knowledge, creating little tutorials. The cattle pages described their particular breeds and gave their history. The unions used old photographs and clippings to make time lines of their histories. Visits by scholars and students will raise the best of these to prominence.

The Internet bug that has bitten museums is good for museums and good for the Grand Idea. The museums benefit from the traffic to their Web sites when they can interest people in visiting their localities and seeing in person the artifacts they learned about online. Along with the artifact exhibits, a museum store usually goes online, adding a profit stream. Museum benefactors savor the lofty and sublime pages showcasing great art, and they are moved to generosity. For the student, the works of Donatello, Rembrandt, and Klee radiate from his desk, and soon, in his hand. Not only that. A student of Rembrandt can simultaneously study the master's paintings from every online museum. In 1992, I flew to Amsterdam to see fifty works by Rembrandt gathered from many museums for an exhibit at the Rijksmuseum. I had to buy my time slot weeks in advance and move with a large number of people through the galleries. The Grand Idea will soon bring everything I could see there into my hand at any time I want to view it. That is sublime. The Rijksmuseum has a gorgeous Web site, by the way; you can choose to read the text in Nederlands, English, Deutsch, Français, Italiano, or Español.

Because the Internet is in its infancy, the Grand Idea is not obvious. Like the baby's conception of a tree, it is not as rich as his or her idea will be in later life, but the connections are valid. The Grand Idea is organic. It grows, and parts of it wither, are pruned, and then refreshed. New twigs of knowledge sprout and develop into branches. Most academic disciplines have already hyperwebbed their ideas to some degree, including mathematicians, herpetologists, biotechnologists, astronomers, linguists, geographers, political scientists and theorists, anthropologists, and so on. Where fields touch each other, they can increasingly be traversed on the Internet, as experts link avenues to exchange what they know. The hyperweb gets richer as mathematical geographers share their formulas with theoretical geometry, as herpetologists and anthropologists find common ideas in the study of migrations.

Two huge forces are maturing the Grand Idea. The first is the cascade of new knowledge onto the Internet, along with advances in cognitive design that make the newer knowledge increasingly instructive and beautiful. The second is the quickening pace of interconnection of related pages and sources. The Grand Idea allows all of us to follow our way through the connections to new understanding and ideas. The echo of the library of Alexandria's destruction need haunt us no more. The knowledge of humankind is converging on the Internet. Its quickening divergence will bring it to everyone on the planet, including all children who hold cheap access to the Grand Idea in their hands.

The Grand Idea is neither a teacher nor a theory. From the perspective of education, the Grand Idea is the substance of what can be taught and known. Many of the biggest battles in education today are fought over theories of how to teach. I think all the theories are essentially correct. If well employed, every method across the spectrum of approaches teaches children, from rows of kids learning by rote to the least confined discovery environment. The Grand Idea is not part of the pedagogical battle. All of the theories of teaching thrive in the new hyper-webbed Grand Idea. Everything is to be found that is set out as a standard for every fifth grader to know; the specifics are all there. Any curriculum or standard is a selection of a few specific things to teach from the knowledge within a field. The U.S. history standard requires knowing about the Civil War but does not include the Spanish-American War. Textbooks are created in the same manner, selecting what pieces of a subject will be taught in what grade at school. A decision is made to teach cell division to sophomores and not to teach trigonometry in high school. Everything to select from for every field of knowledge is available within the Grand Idea, including, of course, the Civil War, the Spanish-American War, cell division, and trigonometry. At the other end of the spectrum of pedagogical theory, constructing learning is quantumly richer than it ever has been when a student is following the organic connections offered among knowledge pages on the Internet. He may start on a page about Hernán Cortéz, notice a link to the Aztecs, and follow his curiosity into constructing an interest in and understanding of Native American history. A child who collects a portfolio over a semester enters the Grand Idea to find a feast of ideas and opportunities to select items for a theme.

Knowledge does not exist for education. Education exists to impart knowledge. What will happen to established education when more and more children around the world hold inexpensive devices in their hands into which they can tune in everything that is known? What will schools be like when their students can move on their own through the elegantly entwined golden radiation of knowledge? I hope your answer is the same as mine: who cares about the schools, the kids are going to be okay! I know it is not that simple, but I am convinced that

the news is that good. The golden horizon has been crossed into the most exciting, creative, and promising of all times to learn and teach. It beckons those of us
in education to accept and enjoy the inescapable adventure of responding to the
Grand Idea.

The sort of grand life my nephews and I glimpsed in the Hamptons is limited
to a few people. Along with private beaches and luxury automobiles, their children can expect to receive a superb education, always a privilege of the elite. An
old tradition among the English upper echelon was the *grand tour*. The term dates
from 1670 and is defined as "an extended tour of the Continent that was formerly
a usual part of the education of young British gentlemen."[7] Throughout history,
in every culture and nation, there have always been a few privileged children to
whom everything that was known was made available. They have been the sons
and daughters of chiefs and kings, despots and tyrants, and the makers and in-
heritors of wealth. No more children will be born into a world where the full
scope of human ideas is accessible only to the elite. Open to all children will be
the grand tour of what is known, as it radiates into their hands. The privilege of
knowledge has ended, and that is digital technology's grandest gift.

NOTES

1. Tim Berners-Lee, *Weaving the Web* (San Francisco: HarperSanFrancisco, 1999), 1–2.

2. *Merriam-Webster's Collegiate Dictionary,* 10th ed., 1997.

3. "Information about Perseus," *Perseus Project* <http://www.perseus.tufts.edu/
PerseusInfo.html>, September 1997 [accessed 3 August 2000].

4. *Archimedes* <http://www.mcs.drexel.edu/~crorres/Archimedes/contents.html>, October 1995 [accessed 3 August 2000].

5. *Stephen Hawking's Website* "Lectures" <http://www.hawking.org.uk/home/hindex.
html> [accessed 3 August 2000].

6. *Intel Museum* <http://www.intel.com/intel/intelis/museum/>, 2000 [accessed 3 August 2000].

7. *Merriam-Webster's Collegiate Dictionary,* 10th ed., 1997.

Index

About the Author

Judy Breck has been actively involved in education since the 1960s. Having taught high school and coached a Texas state champion debate team early in her career, in the 1980s she went on to coordinate the New York based MENTOR program, which established educational partnerships between public schools and law firms. After having built the program as a local project in New York City, she facilitated its expansion nationwide. She also staffed six national Symposia on Partnerships in Education, sponsored by the White House to bring together people and projects striving to improve schools.

With an early effort to leverage the power of the Internet for learning, in the mid 1990s she led the creation of HomeworkCentral, a pioneering educational Web site that organized the educational content of the web for students and researchers. She is currently director of academics at bigchalk.com, an education portal serving the K–12 learning community.